# Hudl

## FOR

# DUMMIES

#### A Wiley Brand

## by Rosemary Hattersley

### FOR

# DUMMIES

#### A Wiley Brand

**Hudl® For Dummies**

Published by
**John Wiley & Sons, Ltd.**
The Atrium
Southern Gate
Chichester
West Sussex
PO19 8SQ
England

Email (for orders and customer service enquires): cs-books@wiley.co.uk

Visit our home page on www.wiley.com

Copyright © 2014 John Wiley & Sons, Ltd, Chichester, West Sussex, England

Published by John Wiley & Sons Ltd, Chichester, West Sussex

For general information on our other products and services, please contact our Customer Care Department within the U.S. at 877-762-2974, outside the U.S. at 317-572-3993, or fax 317-572-4002.

For technical support, please visit www.wiley.com/techsupport.

Wiley also publishes its books in a variety of electronic formats and by print-on-demand. Some content that appears in standard print versions of this book may not be available in other formats. For more information about Wiley products, visit us at www.wiley.com.

British Library Cataloguing in Publication Data: A catalogue record for this book is available from the British Library.

ISBN 978-1-118-90219-6 (pbk); ISBN 978-1-118-90105-2 (ePub)

10  9  8  7  6  5  4  3  2  1

# Contents at a Glance

# Table of Contents

## Chapter 11: Using Your Hudl to Get Organised ......167

## Chapter 12: Shopping on Your Hudl ................183

## Chapter 13: Ten Troubleshooting Tips..............193

## Chapter 14: Ten Ways to Customise Your Hudl ......203

## Index .......................................213

# Introduction

*W*hat is a Hudl? To my mind, it's a family-centric entertainment device that everyone can crowd round, enjoy
together and immediately feel comfortable with.

While writing this book about how to use the Hudl, it certainly
became a fixture in my daily life. It's always there when I want
to check what's on the TV, look up a recipe, find out what the
weather is planning for later in the day or make an impromptu
video when your cousin does something silly. When my tod-
dler nephews came to visit, it was literally child's play to call
up nursery rhymes and interactive storybooks on my Hudl to
keep them enthralled. With the rotten TV reception in my flat,
the Hudl even gives me an extra option for watching live telly,
thanks to a free app that depends on Wi-Fi rather than my TV
signal. I'm sure you'll soon have your own set of everyday
essentials for which your Hudl becomes invaluable.

The Hudl is actually an Android tablet, which means that it's
got Google software and search tools firmly at its heart. The
Hudl makes full use of Google's brilliantly designed Play Store,
which is an online marketplace for music, books, games, films
and software known as *apps*. You can enjoy many of these
entertainment riches for free, and you can also use your Hudl
to play and watch the music, photos and videos you already
own. Because it's so easy to apply content settings, finding
new things to watch and download is never a concern, even
if you hand over the Hudl to a child to use.

One of the first things you'll discover is that the Hudl provides
plenty of help at every turn, thanks to some fantastic screen
tips that help you get started. You'll find shortcuts to sites
you want to go to regularly, whether to download a film or
album or to do your online shopping. You can even use the
Hudl to order your groceries and have them delivered.

Because the Hudl is made exclusively for the UK, everything
about it is set up for UK users. The browser, shopping sites,
film rental, book rental and download services are all set to

show you what's popular in the UK now. The language used to describe how to do things on the Hudl is UK English, and the device automatically uses UK times and dates. It even recognises your location so you don't have to keep typing where you live to find out about the shops and services — or even the train times — that are local to you.

# About This Book

Armed with the tablet's built-in tools and the step-by-step guidance in this book, you'll be up and running with your Hudl in no time. Here's a quick rundown of some of the amazing things you'll be able to do:

- Watch films online for free and download them to watch at your leisure. You can also buy or rent films via your blinkbox or Google account (see Chapter 7).

- Choose a new dress or order your groceries from the comfort of your sofa. Chapter 12 shows you how to browse to any website you like and shop securely.

- Watch BBC iPlayer and programmes on other catch-up TV services. You can even watch live TV, so you don't have to argue over who gets to watch what.

- Find new music online or call up the music that's stored on your computer to listen to on your Hudl without having to transfer it first (see Chapter 8). You just need a Wi-Fi connection to stream your favourite albums.

- Have a phone or video chat with friends around the world; Chapter 5 shows you how. Some great free apps and the Hudl's webcam make this a fun way of keeping in touch.

- Send emails from a Gmail account or any other email address you want to (Chapter 5). Your Hudl is perfect for keeping in touch.

- Keep and manage a diary. Your Hudl has a calendar and can issue reminders about appointments, birthdays and events. Chapter 11 details ways to use the Hudl to help organise your life.

✔ Take photos and videos. After all, the Hudl is a very pocketable device, so you may as well take a snap whenever you see something you want to photograph. You can also store photos you've taken on a digital camera. See Chapter 6.

✔ Edit photos and apply fun effects to them. The Hudl has great editing tools, and you can get even more creative using the apps I introduce you to.

✔ Use your Hudl as a sketchbook (see Chapter 10). You can draw on its touch-sensitive screen by using the tip of your finger or a digital stylus.

✔ Install the latest apps so you can customise your Hudl. The Google Play Store has thousands of games and other ways to entertain you (see Chapter 10).

✔ Check in on Facebook and other social media apps to keep up to date with friends (see Chapter 5).

✔ Find places on a map and get directions on how to get there from home or from your current location (see Chapter 11).

✔ Learn new skills or help your kids with their schoolwork. You can exercise your grey matter, too, with quizzes and brain-training challenges.

✔ Read book after book, including an almost-limitless choice of free classics and children's storybooks.You can download and listen to hundreds of audiobooks as well, as you learn in Chapter 9.

## Foolish Assumptions

I've tried not to make too many assumptions about who might pick up this book, but I assume that you bought a Hudl rather than another type of Android tablet. Although many aspects of the Hudl are based on the Android operating system, lots of extras on the Hudl extend its usefulness.

I also assume that you've already got a wireless Internet connection or are about to start using the web. Like all tablets, the Hudl really comes into its own as a connected device, so web access is absolutely essential. Also, as you'll discover as soon as you start setting up the Hudl, you need web access to create a user account and to log in to it.

# Icons Used in This Book

*Hudl For Dummies, Portable Edition* uses certain art devices to highlight noteworthy items.

 The Tip icon shows something that saves you time or effort or provides a useful workaround. I want you get the most from using your Hudl.

 A Remember item recaps what I just told you, or highlights important new information that you'll want to keep in mind. There's a lot to digest, after all.

 A Technical Stuff passage explains why you need to do something a particular way or use a particular format or setting. Sometimes, it's handy to know what a setting does or why your Hudl behaves as it does.

 Something won't work, or you could damage your Hudl or devices it's attached to, if you don't follow the advice in a Warning paragraph. Most times, however, I use the Warning icon to suggest that you do something in a particular order so that it works first time.

# Where to Go from Here

You need to connect your Hudl to Wi-Fi and decide on some settings before you can start using your Hudl. Chapter 1 gets you started by showing you the controls of your Hudl, and Chapter 2 gets the setup process out the way. After that, your Hudl and its world of entertainment, learning and fun are yours to explore.

# 1

# Finding Your Way Around the Hudl

*Y*ou're ready to dive in and start using your Hudl, but how to begin? In this chapter you take a look at its designs and controls so you know what to tap or press when.

## Checking Out the Specs

The Hudl is a tablet computer that runs the Android mobile operating system. It has a high-resolution 7in touchscreen. Rather than using a keyboard to type what you want to do, you do most things on the Hudl by tapping its screen. Don't worry — the Hudl's screen is pretty resilient and made from scratch-resistant glass, so you won't damage it by tapping it. Because it doesn't have a separate keyboard, the Hudl is very light and small. It weighs just 320g and measures 194x128x11mm.

## Hardware

The Hudl is powered by a quad-core processor and 1GB of RAM. You get 16GB of storage space, which is ample for storing photos, music, videos and books, but you can easily add more storage or copy items to your computer when you don't need them on the Hudl.

Although the Hudl doesn't have a keyboard in the traditional sense, it has an onscreen keyboard that pops up whenever it thinks you need to type something. You'll soon get the hang of using this keyboard, as it's pretty similar to any other keyboard, really, as you see in Chapter 3.

## Software

The Android software includes tools known as *apps* that let you do many things that you might think you'd need a computer for. Accessing the Internet, sending email messages, watching videos, listening to music, having video chats with your nan — you can do all this on your Hudl without needing anything extra. The Hudl is so small and light that you can take it everywhere with you. And because the Hudl is Wi-Fi–enabled and knows where you are at all times, it can tell you things that are relevant to you and your current location.

Your Hudl can do lots of other clever things, too. For some of these things, you'll need to install an app. You discover more about apps in Chapter 3.

Whenever I recommend installing an app, I let you know whether it costs anything and explain how to use it.

# Unboxing Your Hudl

Your Hudl comes in a neat cardboard box with a cable and charger in separate cardboard compartments. The box also contains several bits of paper, which you may be tempted to simply ignore or perhaps throw away.

Those leaflets aren't there to fill otherwise empty space, however. The '123' leaflet (see Figure 1-1), for example, contains useful setup information. It lists the precautions you should take before sharing your Hudl with a child, and describes how to create a passcode to stop anyone else from using your device. It's important to apply a screen lock if you're going to share your Hudl with your children. I look at child-safety issues in detail in Chapter 3.

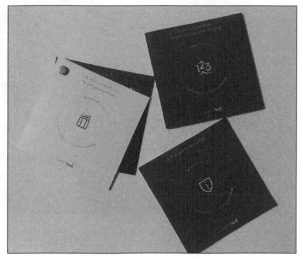

Figure 1-1: The leaflets inside the Hudl's box contain important setup information.

The white-and-blue brochure is a discount booklet that includes a voucher for a year's free broadband Internet access. You'll need Internet access to make full use of your Hudl, so this voucher could come in very useful. The booklet also includes discounts on shopping and entertainment, so it's well worth keeping hold of. You'll be able to take advantage of all these discounts as soon as you've set up your Hudl with a user account and, if you want to, added your Tesco Clubcard details (see Chapter 2).

## Getting to Know the Hudl's Controls

When you first take your Hudl out the box, you'll notice a sheet of transparent plastic on the screen pointing out the locations of some of the most important elements. You won't be able to consult this overlay when you start using the Hudl, however, as it'll get in the way of the touchscreen. The visual guide in Figure 1-2 should help.

let's get you started

Connect to your TV with an HDMI cable and view photos and films on the big screen

Plug your headphones in

SWITCH ON TO START USING

Control the volume

CHARGE YOUR HUDL
Transfer photos and other files via USB

Add more storage with a Micro SD card

Figure 1-2: Get to know the buttons and ports on your Hudl before you begin.

Most of the time, you'll probably use your Hudl in landscape view, as shown in Figure 1-2. Landscape view refers to the Hudl being orientated so that it's suitable for watching a film or TV programme, rather than scrolling up and down the pages of a book. Because the Hudl has a sensor inside, it knows which way is up, and the display rotates accordingly, so it doesn't really matter which way round you hold it.

Nonetheless, the Hudl does have a definite top and a bottom. You can tell which is the top when you're holding the Hudl in landscape view, because there's a small dot in the middle of the black bezel along one long edge. This dot is actually the lens of the Hudl's front camera, which also serves as a webcam for video calls.

If you hold the Hudl in both hands and bring it towards you, you'll see your face reflected in the screen. The dot for the camera should correspond with your forehead.

The next things to notice are the two skinny buttons on the Hudl's right edge (see Figure 1-3). These buttons are the only hardware buttons the Hudl has. Everything else is controlled via its touchscreen, as you see in Chapter 3. The top button is the power button. Gently press and hold it for a moment to turn the device on and off — a deliberate feature that stops you accidentally switching the Hudl on or off while it's in your bag. If the Hudl is in standby mode, press the power button to make the screen switch on.

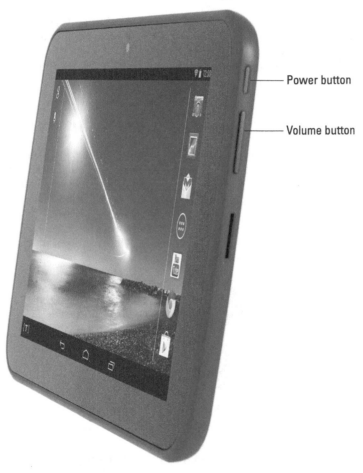

Power button

Volume button

Figure 1-3: The only controls on the Hudl's case are the power and volume buttons.

The button below the power button is much longer; it's actually a rocker that adjusts the volume. Press the top portion of this button to make the volume louder, and press the bottom portion of this button to make it quieter. If you hold either part of this button down, the volume continues to increase or decrease, whereas pressing it once changes the volume by a fraction.

If you've got headphones plugged in and try to make the volume go all the way up to its maximum, a message appears onscreen, asking whether you really want it to be so loud. It's a thoughtful touch to be asked whether you want to do something that might harm your hearing.

## Storing things on your Hudl

Below the volume button on the right edge of the Hudl is a sizable recess, which is the micro-SD card slot. Your Hudl has 16GB (gigabytes) of storage already, but you can use a micro-SD card like the one shown in Figure 1-4 to add even more. The device can accept micro-SD cards that hold up to 32GB of storage, so you can store a total 48GB of 'stuff' on your Hudl — enough to store thousands of photos or dozens of Hollywood movies.

Figure 1-4: You can insert a micro-SD card like this one into the slot on the right edge of the Hudl.

You'll probably want to use the micro-SD card slot if you've taken a set of photos on your digital camera or smartphone and want to transfer those photos to your Hudl quickly so you can view them on its beautiful screen.

# Connecting and charging your Hudl

Moving to the bottom edge of the Hudl, you'll find another slot midway along its length. This slot is the charging point for the Hudl. The cable that comes with your Hudl has a USB connector at one end and a smaller micro-USB connector at the other end (see Figure 1-5). Plug the USB-connector end into the port of the mains adapter when you want to charge your Hudl, and slot the micro-USB end of the cable into the port at the bottom of the Hudl, keeping the ridged side of the silver connector uppermost.

Figure 1-5: Make sure that you have the ridged side of the micro-USB connector uppermost when plugging it into the Hudl.

You can also use the micro-USB port on your Hudl to connect the Hudl to a laptop or computer or to a digital camera or external speakers. When connected to a laptop or computer using the micro-USB connection, your Hudl will charge, but it won't draw as much power as when charging from the mains and will therefore charge very slowly.

Because your Hudl probably wasn't fully charged when you took it out of the box, I suggest you set it to charge now while you find out more about what your new device can do.

Your Hudl should last for about nine hours before its battery needs to be recharged. The battery lasts longer if the Hudl isn't being used intensively or if it spends time sitting in standby mode (see the nearby sidebar 'Putting your Hudl on hold'). Recharging the Hudl from scratch takes around 2.5 hours.

The Hudl's battery depletes faster if it's constantly using the Internet to show videos and play music. The Wi-Fi connection uses battery power to transfer information from the Internet to the Hudl, and playing music and video makes the Hudl's processor work hard. If you want to watch a high-definition film, it can be better to download it to your Hudl, rather than stream it over a Wi-Fi connection. I explain how to do this in Chapter 7.

It's best not to leave your Hudl charging all the time, as this will eventually make the battery last less long. You'll get an onscreen message when the Hudl's battery is getting a bit low. Unless you're going to use the Hudl all day without charging it, wait until you see the low-battery message before plugging it in.

## Putting your Hudl on hold

Standby mode is useful because it allows the Hudl to come back to life almost instantly when you tap the power button. This means you don't have to wait while the Hudl powers up.

As long as the battery wasn't critically low when you last used it, you can leave the Hudl in standby mode for a day or two, and it will still have enough power for you to use it again.

Standby mode uses a tiny amount of power. It does use *some* power, however, so make sure you fully power down the Hudl if you're not going to use it for a few days.

## Making audio and video connections

Your Hudl has three more ports, each of which is related to entertainment:

- ✓ **Micro-HDMI port:** The micro-HDMI port is on the top edge of the device, slightly to the left of centre. You use this port when you want to attach your Hudl to a device that can play high-definition video (see Chapter 7).

- ✓ **Headphone jack:** The round slot on the top-right edge of your Hudl is one that you'll probably recognise from other gadgets you've used. It's the headphone jack (see Figure 1-6). Just plug in any headphones or earphones you like, and you'll be able to listen to music and play games or videos on your Hudl without anyone interrupting you.

Headphone jack

Figure 1-6: You'll find the Hudl's entertainment-related connections on its top edge.

As I note earlier in this chapter, the Hudl displays a warning if you try to crank up the volume while you've got your headphones plugged in. This screen warning is especially helpful if you'd like your child to be able to use the Hudl. You can plug in the child's headphones and know that the volume won't be too loud. If you've got really young children, I suggest getting them a pair of volume-limiting headphones. See Chapter 14 for recommendations.

✔ **Microphone:** The tiny hole next to the headphone jack is the microphone, which you use when chatting to friends online or in a video call. The microphone also picks up the sound of your voice when you're recording memos (see Chapter 11), dictating an email (see Chapter 3) and giving the Hudl verbal instructions. Yes, you can get your Hudl to help you with your homework by asking it to find facts for you online.

# Exploring the Rear of the Hudl

The back of the Hudl is covered by a nonslip material that also prevents it from getting — or leaving — scratches. In the centre, you see the metallic *hudl* lettering, as shown in Figure 1-7. Below it is the Tesco logo, and farther down are reference codes relating to the Hudl's design.

At the top right (if you're viewing the Hudl's rear) is the main camera, which sits slightly proud of the rest of the case. The camera can capture 3mp (megapixels) of detail; it can also record 720p video. For best results, make sure there's plenty of light — and don't cover the lens! You look at taking photos and recording videos in Chapter 6.

Finally, you find metallic strips two thirds of the way down the case on either side. You may think that these strips are supposed to be grips, and you could certainly use them for this purpose. In fact, they're the grilles for the Hudl's stereo speakers. When you've got some music on your Hudl (see Chapter 8), you'll find out just how good the audio setup of your Hudl is.

Camera

Figure 1-7: The back of the Hudl lists important technical information about your Hudl, as well as housing the main camera.

# Powering Up Your Hudl

After you've familiarised yourself with the Hudl's buttons, ports and switches and given it a chance to charge, it's time to switch it on for the first time. Press and hold the power button on the right until the star appears onscreen. Voila!

In Chapter 2, I go through everything you need to know about setting up the Hudl. You need a Wi-Fi connection in order to complete the setup process.

It's most comfortable to hold the Hudl in both hands so that the screen is in landscape mode (as though you're watching a video on it). Make sure that the front camera is pointing at your forehead rather than your chin.

# 2
# Setting Up Your Hudl

*Y*our Hudl is designed to be easy to use. Setting it up for the first time takes only a few minutes. There are plenty of prompts to make sure things are set up safely and securely as you go. I make it clear in this chapter wherever there's a setting you may want to change or an issue to consider. I also show you how to set up your Hudl so that it can be used safely by anyone in the family.

Setting up your Hudl for the first time is easy if you've already got a Gmail address, but there's no need to worry if you haven't used email before; I show you how to create and send emails. You will also need to have wireless Internet access.

Make sure that you've charged up your Hudl before you set out. Chapter 1 describes how to charge the Hudl.

## *Switching It On*

To switch it on, hold your Hudl in both hands with the screen in landscape mode, as though you were watching TV on it. Grip the sides of the Hudl with your thumbs about halfway up, and extend your index fingers. The Hudl should end up cradled in your palms. Check that the front-facing camera (the dot in the black bezel around the screen) is at the top. Now run your right index finger up and down the right edge of the Hudl. You should feel two buttons. Firmly press the upper button. Keep holding it down until a white star appears in the middle of the screen. After a couple of seconds, the star is replaced by the word *Hudl*.

After about a minute, you see an onscreen message like the one in Figure 2-1, suggesting that you set up your Hudl. Tap Start to begin.

Figure 2-1: You'll see a friendly greeting when you switch on your Hudl for the first time.

# Connecting to Wi-Fi

Before you can go any further, you have to connect your Hudl to the Internet over a stable Wi-Fi connection. By stable I mean a connection that doesn't suddenly disappear. You need this connection to register your Google and Tesco accounts and to ensure your Hudl's software and apps are kept up to date.

After you turn on your Hudl, it looks for available Wi-Fi connections and displays a list of any wireless networks it finds. The strongest Wi-Fi signal is shown at the top of the list, with weaker signals farther down, as shown in Figure 2-2. The stronger a connection is, the more white bars the fan denoting the connection has.

Figure 2-2: If several wireless networks are available, choose the one near the top of the list, as it has a strong signal — but make sure it has a padlock icon to show that it's secure.

To connect your Hudl to Wi-Fi, follow these steps:

1. **Tap the name of the Wi-Fi network that you want to use.**

   Unless the wireless connection is your own, you should connect only to a network that has a padlock icon next it. The padlock icon shows that the connection is secure and requires a password to connect to it. I cover staying safe with Wi-Fi in detail in Chapter 4.

   If you know the password, tap in the password entry box. A keyboard appears at the bottom half of the screen.

2. **Type the password for the network. Passwords usually consist of upper- and lowercase letters as well as numbers. Passwords are case-sensitive, so your password will be rejected if you type 'T' as 't', for example.**

   If you need to type a number, tap the ?123 button in the bottom left of the keyboard to change to the numerical keyboard. To change back to the alphabetical keyboard, tap the button in the same location, which is now labelled ABC.

 Sometimes, the Wi-Fi network details are displayed on the wall or on the menu at a cafe. If not, politely ask a member of staff (or another customer) for the name and password of the Wi-Fi network.

3. **Tick Continue on the next screen to confirm that you agree to use your Hudl properly.**

   These terms and conditions state that you won't hack other people's tablets or computers or copy the software the Hudl runs on.

4. **On the Wi-Fi and Location screen, set your location options; then tap the grey arrow at the bottom right of the screen to continue.**

   This screen contains details about why it's a good idea to let Google and Google's apps use your Wi-Fi location. Tap to untick any options you aren't comfortable with.

 Google and many other available apps want to be able to use your Wi-Fi location so they can show you where the nearest shops, stations and places are. This feature is especially useful for giving you directions and for ensuring that you get information that's relevant to the UK, rather than to the United States or other countries. Google doesn't save this information anywhere. If you don't like the idea of location information being made available to these services, just untick the boxes.

# Setting Up a Google Account

The next step is setting up your Google account. Follow these steps:

1. **In the Set Up Google? screen (see Figure 2-3), do one of the following:**

   • Tap OK and proceed to Step 2.

   • Tap No Thanks and skip to 'Setting Up Your Tesco Account' later in this chapter.

If you tap No Thanks, you get the option to log in to or create a Tesco account so you can use the shopping and entertainment services that are included on your Hudl. If you don't set up a Google account you can still use your Hudl to surf the web, listen to music, and take and view photos and videos on the Hudl itself, but you won't be able to use it to buy or download apps, music, games, films and books from the Google Play Store.

Figure 2-3: Setting up a Google account lets you download and buy apps, games and music from the Google Play Store.

2. **In the next screen, tap New to set up a Google account, Existing if you've got a Google account already or Not Now if you don't want to set up a Google account at the moment.**

   The Hudl uses your Google account details when you buy anything at the Google Play Store. You therefore need a Google account to buy and download apps, games, music, films and books to use on your Hudl. You can use a different email address later, if you want.

3. **Do one of the following:**

   • If you're setting up a Google account for the first time, type your first and last names in the appropriate fields and then tap Next.

   This name appears on your Hudl's 'owner' page and also appears as the sender's name when you email people. The account you're about to create gives you an email address that ends in @gmail.com.

• If you've used an Android device before or have an account on YouTube (which Google owns), you'll already have a login you can use on your Hudl. Sign in using your existing login information. You can then skip forward to 'Adding or declining optional Google services' later in this chapter to continue setting up your Hudl.

4. **Enter a username, and tap the grey arrow onscreen.**

Your username doesn't have to be based on your actual name, but it may be easier for you to remember if it is. Unlike the owner-name details that you entered in Step 3, the username for the Google account can't be altered.

Google checks its records to see whether another Google user has already chosen that name. If the name is unavailable, you see the message *'Username' isn't available.* Tap the down arrow below the keyboard to make the keyboard disappear, and you see the message *Touch for suggestions.* Tap this message to bring up a list of available usernames based on what you typed (see Figure 2-4). Tap to select one of these suggestions or type another username.

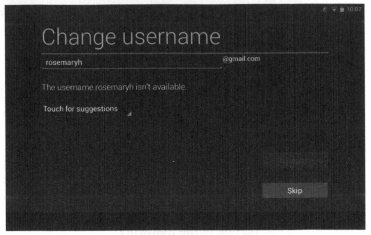

Figure 2-4: It's not easy to think up original usernames, but your Hudl can suggest some.

5. **When you've got a unique username, tap the grey arrow onscreen or tap Done on the onscreen keyboard.**

# Creating a secure password

The next screen asks you to choose a password. Type a password of at least eight characters. It's best to choose a password that contains a combination of upper- and lowercase letters and includes at least one numeral.

Don't make the password something that's easy to guess, such as the name of your favourite football or cricket team.

The password field may be obscured by the Create Password page heading. If you turn your Hudl through 90 degrees so you're looking at it more like a book, the password field becomes visible.

Below the password field is a message stating whether the password is too short, fair or strong. Ideally, you want to create a strong password, which means it's hard to guess. You may not need to change a 'fair' password much to make it a 'strong' one. The password ryangiggs was rated fair, for example, but RyanGiggs was strong.

When you have a strong password, tap Next and then type the password again on the next line to confirm it.

# Setting recovery information

After you have your password, you need to set some recovery information for use if you ever forget the password for your Google account. To do so, follow these steps:

1. **In the Recovery Information screen, tap Choose a Security Question.**

   A list of questions appears (see Figure 2-5).

2. **Tap the security question that you'd like to use.**

   The answers to some questions may be easy for other people to guess, so try to avoid using those questions. On the other hand, will you really remember your first-ever phone number under pressure?

3. **Type the answer to your chosen security question and tap the grey arrow to continue.**

4. **Enter an alternative email address where you can pick up your recovery password link.**

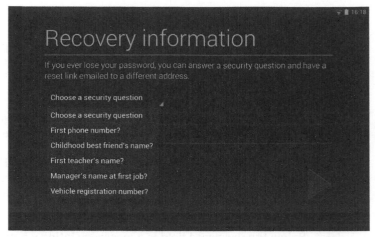

Figure 2-5: Choose a security question that you can answer if you lose your password.

You can request a recovery password by tapping Forgot Password under the sign-in fields for your Google account. If you ask for a recovery password, Google sends a message to this email address; you reply to this message to confirm your identity.

If you don't have another email address you can use, enter the email address of a very trustworthy friend or family member. First, however, ask them whether it's all right to use their address as your alternative email address.

I recommend that as soon as you finish setting up your Hudl, you set up a second email address that you can use in an emergency. Then go back to the settings in your Google account and change the email address where Google will send the recovery link.

## Adding or declining optional Google services

When you finish setting up your Google account, you'll be offered the option to set up more Google services. The same email address and user account details are used for them all, which is why it's very important that you keep your login details secret.

## Finalising account settings

On the Finish Account screen, you can choose whether or not to turn on web history — which is useful for finding web pages you've visited before — and get emails about Google Play. Google Play is where you usually go whenever you want to add apps, games and other content to your Hudl. Untick these options if you prefer, and then tap the grey arrow.

On the Authenticating screen, type the bunched-up letters you see. This so-called *CAPTCHA* image is hard to see because of the page design, so turn the Hudl to portrait (book-reading) mode, and you'll be able to see the text and instructions clearly.

The last choice you need to make is whether to have the tablet backed up along with your Google account. I recommend keeping this option ticked because then everything you do on your Hudl (but not the items you create on it) is kept safe. If you were ever to lose your Hudl, you'd be able to retrieve everything that was stored in your Google account.

# Setting Up Your Tesco Account

Your Hudl comes with a purpose built Tesco groceries app that makes shopping a breeze. The option to add a Tesco account appears after you've finished setting up your Google account. Here's how to set up a Tesco account:

1. **Do one of the following:**

   • If you've already registered your Clubcard, tap Yes on the Have a Tesco Account? screen (see Figure 2-6) and type the email address and password you use for the account. Once you've signed in, your Hudl will complete its setup process by checking for any updates to the apps and Android operating system installed on it.

   • If you don't have a Tesco account, tap No and then tap Register on the next screen (or tap Skip This Step for Now instead, if you prefer). Then proceed to Step 2.

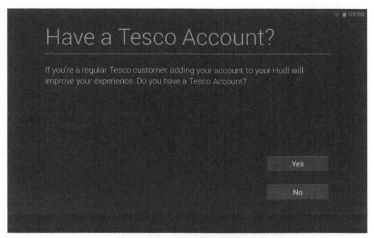

Figure 2-6: If you're a regular Tesco customer, it makes sense to add your account to your Hudl so you can easily order goods and check your Clubcard balance.

2. **To register for a new Tesco account, type your name, email address, postcode and Tesco Clubcard number (if you have one); then tap Done.**

   Your Hudl saves all your details. After about 30 seconds, you should see the message shown in Figure 2-7.

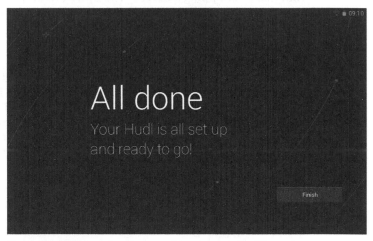

Figure 2-7: When you've set everything up, your Hudl is ready to go.

# Sharing Your Hudl with a Child

Your Hudl is fantastic for sharing with family members, but because it lets you surf the web and watch films, you should make sure you apply settings that let youngsters view only age-appropriate content.

As soon as your Hudl is set up, a screen appears asking whether you intend to share your Hudl with a child (see Figure 2-8). Just tap the Get Advice button to see useful information about what you should consider when allowing a child to use your Hudl. In Chapter 3, I explain which settings to use to make your Hudl child-friendly.

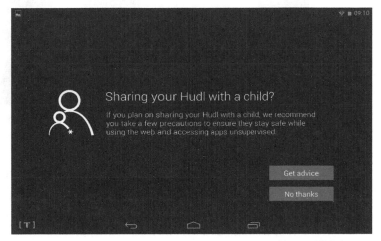

**Figure 2-8:** Make sure that you read the advice about letting a child use your Hudl.

When you've finished reading the child safety advice, tap OK to move on to screens explaining how to start using your Hudl. When you've finished reading these, tap OK and you will arrive at the Home screen.

# Getting Started with the Hudl

The Home screen, shown in Figure 2-9, has a coastal scene in the background, a vertical set of icons on the right and a large Getting Started box in the middle of the screen. This Getting

Started app is exclusive to the Hudl and invaluable for getting the most from it. Tap Let's Go to find out more about music, photos, games, messaging and the other features of your Hudl. This useful feature provides lots of details about how to start using your tablet.

Figure 2-9: The Getting Started app is a great place to start finding out what your Hudl can do.

At the bottom of the screen, you see a [T] button, which takes you to the Tesco World app. This button is always available on your Hudl. Tap it to go straight to Tesco services, including blinkbox music, movies and books and to go to the Tesco Direct website and Tesco Groceries app.

The final introductory screen highlights the All Apps icon. When you start using your Hudl, you'll probably find it useful to arrange your apps so that only the most frequently used ones appear on your Home screen. I look at how to manage your apps in Chapter 3.

Your Hudl's screen will dim and its screen will lock if you don't touch it for a few minutes. To reawaken the Hudl, press the power button at the top right edge of the device and then put your finger on the padlock icon that appears. Swipe your finger across the screen from the locked padlock to the unlocked padlock to unlock your tablet so you can use it again.

# Keeping Your Hudl Secure

You'll probably want to take your Hudl everywhere with you. But because it's so light and portable, it's easy to mislay; under a cushion on the sofa is where I often find mine. If you lose it somewhere outside the home, you'll be kicking yourself. Fortunately, you can lessen the blow by making sure that no one else can get at anything you've stored on it or read your emails.

The first step in securing your Hudl is adding a passcode, which will stop anyone — including your kids — from using it. To add a passcode, follow these steps:

1. **Press the top-right corner of the screen and then drag down until a menu appears.**

2. **Tap Settings.**

3. **Scroll down to the Security section (below Personal).**

   The first entry in this section is Screen Lock, which by default is set to Slide Underneath. This setting means that anyone who picks up your Hudl needs only slide his or her finger across the screen to unlock it.

4. **Tap Screen Lock to change the setting.**

5. **On the Choose Screen Lock page, tap a security option.**

   For purposes of this exercise, tap Pattern.

6. **A grid of dots appears. Swipe your finger to create a pattern of dots (see Figure 2-10).**

   When you've finished, the words 'Pattern Recorded' appear above the grid. Tap Continue to proceed. On the next screen repeat the pattern to confirm it.

If you prefer, you can choose a different Screen Lock option in Step 5. Just draw the pattern you chose in Step 6 to make any changes.

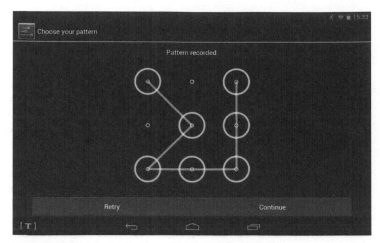

Figure 2-10: Make your Hudl secure by adding a PIN or pattern.

It's possible to use your own face as a security option. If you tap this option in Step 5 and then tap Set It Up, the Hudl's camera will launch and take a photo of you. This security method isn't as secure as using a PIN or passcode, so we recommend using one of these options instead.

In Chapter 3, I provide more details on keeping your Hudl secure, and I also cover how you and your child(ren) can use the web safely.

# 3

# Exploring the Hudl

*M*ost things you do on your Hudl use the touch-sensitive screen. At first glance, it seems as though the screen has no controls or buttons. It does, though. The controls are just hidden from view until you need to use them. That way, you can use the whole screen for viewing web pages, photos, videos, games and the pages of books. This minimalist approach limits distractions. Another cunning thing about the Hudl is that it has several Home screen views you can move between. You can use these screens to arrange items so you can find them easily.

Your Hudl can do almost anything that a computer can, but the one big difference is that the Hudl has no physical keyboard. As I discuss in Chapter 2, the Hudl has an onscreen keyboard that appears only when you need to type something. You can make it appear on demand, however, and change which keys are available.

You can launch most tasks on your Hudl by tapping to launch an *app* — a small application or dedicated program designed specifically for that task. In this chapter, I introduce the apps that come preinstalled on the Hudl and the extras that you won't find on other Android tablets.

Many of the things you do on your Hudl involve using the web, so I look in detail at how to navigate to websites and how to get around the Internet from your Hudl. I also discuss settings and precautions you may want to put in place before letting your kids loose with your Hudl.

# Getting to Know the Hudl's Controls

The Hudl's screen goes blank whenever you haven't tapped it for a few minutes — an arrangement that preserves the battery. To make the screen active again, push the power button on the top-right edge of the Hudl; then, when the lock screen appears (see Figure 3-1), put your index finger on the lock icon and slide it to the right and onto the unlock icon.

**Figure 3-1:** After a few minutes of inactivity, your Hudl's screen goes blank. Unlock it by pressing the power button and then sliding your finger across the screen.

When you unlock your Hudl, you'll probably see the Home screen. The Hudl launches to this screen by default unless you stop doing something on your Hudl momentarily and then return to it. You can get back to the Home screen by tapping the house icon at the bottom-centre of the screen.

You initiate most actions by tapping an item to open it or to select the option you want. In some cases, you also need to tap an onscreen button to confirm your choice. Often, there's a menu at the top right or top left of the screen. You may need to tap the screen to get the menu to appear. It will either be indicated by a stack of horizontal lines or as a vertical bar composed of several dots. Other menus sometimes appear if you tap and hold your finger on an option for a while. If nothing happens after a few seconds, no additional options are available or you've tapped the wrong place.

To get a closer view of a photo or an article on a website, you zoom in by quickly tapping the screen twice. You can also zoom into photos by placing your thumb and forefinger on the Hudl's screen and moving them apart. Double-tap the screen to make the photo revert to its usual size.

## Navigating the Hudl's screens

The Home screen is where the most important functions are housed. The Home screen on your Hudl is not only one window, though. In total, the Hudl has five screens.

### Moving from screen to screen

To move between these screens, just put your finger on the Hudl's screen and swipe from left to right. You should see two more screens when you swipe to the left and two additional screens when you swipe to the right.

You know when you reach the final screen because the edge of the screen glows bright blue and appears to lift up.

At the moment, these other screens have got links to some of the Tesco-owned services you can use with your Hudl (see Figure 3-2). You can move or remove these links, however, and put anything you want on these screens. Use these screens to organise everything on your Hudl as you want. You might have one screen for everything related to entertainment; another for keeping in touch by email, social media and phone; and yet another for your organisational tools.

Figure 3-2: Swipe right or left to see the Hudl's five screens and the Tesco services you can launch directly from them.

### Moving items between screens

To move an item elsewhere on the same screen, place and hold your finger on the icon you want to move and drag the icon to its new position. Take your finger off the screen, and the icon stays in its new location. To move an icon to a different screen, select it by placing your finger on it; then drag it to the extreme right or left of the screen to move it one screen either side of its original location.

You can move apps and *widgets* (the larger items that look like sticky notes) between screens. You can also remove an app or widget by holding your finger down on the item you want to get rid of until an X appears in the top-left corner. Drag the item to be removed to the top-left corner of the screen so it's on top of the X. When the app or widget turns red, let go or flick the item off the top of the screen. Not everything can be removed this way, but many items can. I look at more ways to customise your Hudl and organise what's on your screen in Chapters 11 and 12.

## *Making hidden navigation buttons appear*

One great thing about the Hudl is that you can have lots of things on the go at once, but if you tap the Home button (the house icon at the bottom of the screen), you can immediately suspend all those activities and do something else, such as looking up a TV actor online before continuing to watch the film he's in.

If you can't see the Home button at the bottom of the screen, it's probably because an app is running or something is playing, and the Hudl has hidden everything away so it doesn't distract you. To make the Home button appear, just tap the bottom portion of the screen. In some apps (such as the Gallery photo viewer, shown in Figure 3-3), you can make the Home button reappear by tapping anywhere on the screen.

Home button

Figure 3-3: If the Home button disappears from the bottom of the screen, tap anywhere to make it reappear.

The back-arrow to the left of the Home button is the Back button. Tapping this button takes you back to whatever was onscreen immediately before the screen you're looking at now. It's useful when you're setting things up and want to check what you've just done or the information you typed. The Back button can also be useful if you accidentally jump to another app or web page and just want to go back to where you were (but don't want to stop whatever task you were just doing).

There's one more button you can access from the bottom of the screen. If you hold your finger on the Home screen button, a white circle with the word Google appears. This button is for Google Now, which uses information from your Google accounts and your location details to provide up to the minute travel, weather and news. Tap 'Yes I'm In' if you want to make use of Google Now.

## Checking what's running on your Hudl

The third icon at the bottom of the screen — the overlapping rectangles — is the Recents button. It shows you everything that's happening on your Hudl. Whenever you tap this button, you see a scrollable filmstrip of the tasks you've got open, from web pages and half-written emails to the photo gallery and so on. Use your finger to scroll left and right through each of these items you have running. Tap any one of them to make the current screen the active screen and continue where you left off.

If you find that you've forgotten you had something open, you can easily close it. Just hold your finger on the small filmstrip image of it and then flick up or down to dismiss it (see Figure 3-4). That item closes and disappears from view. Don't worry — you won't have deleted anything. The item is automatically saved at the point where it was last used.

Figure 3-4: Dismiss anything you no longer want to have open by holding its thumbnail and then flicking up or down.

## Using the Hudl's Getting Started app

In the middle of the Home screen is a really useful app labelled Getting Started. It contains lots of useful information about how to get the most from your Hudl, and I really recommend you make use of it.

Tap Let's Go to launch Getting Started. As you read each screen, you're offered new information about various aspects of your Hudl. If you prefer to pick and choose what you see first, just tap the 123 icon in the top-left corner of the Getting Started app. A menu appears, giving you access to Hudl Basics, Child Safety, Essential Apps and information about the entertainment options you can enjoy on your Hudl (see Figure 3-5). Many of these options are specific to the Hudl, so it's worth going through each of these sections to see what you might otherwise miss out on.

Figure 3-5: The Getting Started app explains what the Hudl can do and suggests ways of doing them.

The Getting Started app is preinstalled on the Hudl and is always available if you want to check how to do something (and don't have this book to hand). To launch the Getting Started app manually, tap the Let's Go button on the widget pre-installed on the Home screen of your Hudl.

Because the Getting Started app bookmarks how far you've got through it, you should see something new each time you use it. If you want to go through it at your own pace or go over ground you've already covered, just tap the 123 icon at the top left to see the chapter list, or tap the menu at the top right to reset it.

# Exploring the Favourites Bar

Down the right side of the each screen is a row of icons that launch some of the items you're likely to use frequently. This row of icons is the *Favourites bar* (see Figure 3-6). No matter which of the Hudl's five screens you're on, the Favourites bar will always be on the right edge. It isn't visible when you're using apps.

Here's what each of the icons in the Favourites bar launches (from top to bottom):

- **Camera:** As you'd expect, tapping this icon launches the Hudl's main camera. The Hudl has a 3MP camera on the rear and a 2MP camera on the front). You can switch between cameras whenever you like. For details of how to use the Camera app, see Chapter 6.

- **Gallery:** The next icon down looks like a picture frame. This icon opens the Gallery — the place where you'll find your photos, screen shots and any images that someone sends you and that you decide to save to your Hudl. Any videos you record on your Hudl also appear in the Gallery. (I look at how to make the most of the photo viewer in Chapter 6.)

- **Email:** Next in the Favourites bar is the Email app. If you set up a new email account on your Hudl as I discuss in Chapter 2, your emails appear here. As with most things on your Hudl, you simply tap to open the Email app. Things are slightly different if you're using a Google email address as you need to open the Gmail app to get to your emails. You'll find the Gmail icon by tapping the next icon down (see the next item).

✔ **All Apps:** Tapping the circular icon in the Favourites bar takes you to a multiple-screen grid showing all the apps and widgets installed on your Hudl (see Figure 3-7). Many icons make it sufficiently clear what the app is or what it does; each icon is also labelled.

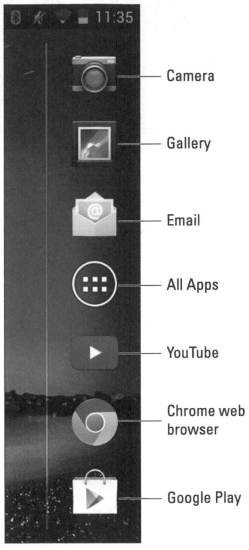

11:35

Camera

Gallery

Email

All Apps

YouTube

Chrome web browser

Google Play

Figure 3-6: Items that you'll want to access all the time are stored in the Favourites bar.

Figure 3-7: In the All Apps screen, you can view all the apps and widgets on your Hudl.

Broadly speaking, *apps* are used to perform specific tasks or run a particular service, whereas *widgets* add functionality to the Hudl itself.

To see all the apps that are already installed on your Hudl, put your finger on the screen and swipe from side to side. To see the widgets that are on your Hudl, tap the Widgets tab above the apps grid. Again, if you swipe from left to right, you can see the complete selection. I look at how to make use of widgets and how to find and install more apps later in this chapter.

✔ **YouTube:** The three bottom icons on the Favourites bar are for web-based apps. The big red Play button is for YouTube, the free online video channel that anyone can contribute to. To learn about watching TV and videos on your Hudl, see Chapter 7.

✔ **Chrome:** Below the YouTube icon is the icon for Chrome, Google's web browser. Tap this icon whenever you want to go online.

✔ **Google Play:** Finally, the icon at the bottom is for Google Play. Tapping this icon takes you to the Google Play Store, where you can buy or download books, apps, music, videos and TV programmes. You can also see anything you've purchased or downloaded for free here. I look at how to buy apps from Google Play at the end of this chapter.

# Exploring the Hudl's Links

The buttons along the left edge of the screen are links rather than apps in their own right. Here's how to use them.

## Google

At the top is the g icon, which stands for Google. Tap this icon to start a web search. You can search for almost anything, from a website to a literary quote. Try to be as specific as possible.

Regardless of what you type in the search field, Google looks for matching items online (as long as you've got a web connection) and tries to second-guess what you want it to find for you, as shown in Figure 3-8. Google also looks for search matches on your Hudl among your apps, your emails and the titles of any books, films and songs you've got.

**Figure 3-8:** Google tries to work out what you want it to search for and lists suggestions you can tap to select.

 You'll notice that Google also displays your most recent searches. If you begin typing something that seems to match a search you've done before, Google lists this item below the search field as a suggestion. Tap the item to go straight to that search.

If your search doesn't yield exactly what you're after, you can search again by using slightly different search terms. Tap the original search term, and hold your finger on the arrow at the end of the search term. Similar searches appear in the suggestions list. These suggestions are based on popular searches that other people have tried. Using a popular search term can make it quicker to find what you want online.

## Speech recognition

Below the Google icon at the top left of the Hudl's screen is the microphone icon. Tap the microphone to launch Google's speech-recognition tool, which you can use to tell Google what you want to search for. The speech-recognition tool is useful in all sorts of situations, such as getting directions when you're driving or finding recipe instructions when your hands are covered in goo. The tool recognizes common instructions such as 'Set alarm', 'Note to self' and 'Directions to . . . '.

Just tap the microphone at the top right of the screen to make Google start listening. What Google thinks you said appears onscreen. Assuming that Google understood you correctly, after a couple of seconds, you see the answer to your question or the result of your instruction (see Figure 3-9).

**Figure 3-9:** Tap the microphone icon whenever you want to give Google verbal instructions.

## Tesco

The [T] icon at the bottom left of the Hudl's screen is a permanent link to all things Tesco. By tapping this icon, you can go straight to the Tesco services you want to use, such as the online grocery store service, the Tesco website and dedicated blinkbox music, TV, book and film services. I look at how to use each of these services, as well as other sites in Chapters 7, 8, 9 and 12. As you see in Figure 3-10, when you first tap the [T] icon, you're shown how to find each item.

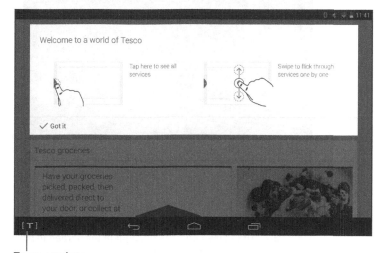

Tesco services

Figure 3-10: Tap the [T] icon to go straight to your Clubcard account details and Tesco services.

# Finding the Hudl's Hidden Menus

The Hudl has two menus that don't have icons to launch them. The first such menu is the Quick Settings menu. To make this menu appear, place a finger near the top right of the Hudl's screen and hold your finger on the screen as you drag downwards. A grid like the one in Figure 3-11 should appear, showing how much battery charge your Hudl has left and what connections are active. You can also access your Hudl's Settings menu when you're creating additional user accounts and changing security settings on your Hudl.

The other hidden menu — Notifications — is at the top left of the Hudl's screen. You get a notification in the form of a tiny envelope icon whenever a new email arrives in your inbox. You also see notifications about other events, such as when a photo is saved or when you connect your Hudl to something else, such as your laptop. Drag the Notifications menu down to see a preview of the latest message or event (see Figure 3-12). To view an email in full, just tap it, and your Hudl opens your email inbox. Tap the series of white rectangles at the top right of the Notifications menu to dismiss all notifications.

Figure 3-11: Drag down from the top right of the screen to make the Quick Settings menu appear.

Figure 3-12: Pull down the Notifications menu to preview recently delivered emails or view events.

# Mastering Your Hudl's Keyboard

Whenever you need to type something, a keyboard appears in the bottom half of the screen. Because the Hudl's screen is large, you should find it just as easy to tap the right keys whether the Hudl is held in portrait or landscape mode. The keyboard automatically rotates so that it's the right way up. Spelling suggestions appear above the keyboard as you type. If you aren't a speedy typist, tap a word that the Hudl suggests to save time. When you finish typing, tap the Enter key (the left arrow).

Sometimes, instead of displaying an arrow, the Enter key displays a word, such as *Done* or *Go*.

If the keyboard doesn't disappear when you want it to, tap the down button at the bottom of the screen next to the Home button. To make it reappear, just tap anywhere you usually type text.

If you need to type a number or a character that isn't shown on the keyboard's screen, tap the ?123 button at bottom left (see Figure 3-13). The keyboard changes to show numbers rather than letters, as well as lots of useful symbols, including the all-important @ sign used in email addresses. There's also a dedicated symbols keyboard that you can invoke by tapping the ~[< key on the extreme left or right side of the numeric keyboard. If you want to personalise your emails tap the 'smiley' icon at the bottom right, and explore the range of emoticons and graphics you can add to your message.

Some keys have small dots next to them, indicating that you can access other options if you hold down your finger on those keys. Tapping the microphone key at the bottom left of the keyboard in the Email app or to the right of the search box in Google starts the speech-recognition tool, which you can use to dictate messages to your Hudl (see Figure 3-14). If you tap and hold the microphone key in the Email app, the input options appear. Tap Input Languages to change the language and keys the Hudl displays. Tap Google Keyboard Settings to see the currently selected options. You see that by default, the Hudl is set not to suggest offensive words.

Another useful option is Gesture Typing, which is already active on your Hudl. To use this option, just glide your finger from one letter to another on the keyboard rather than tapping them individually. You will see a white line follow the path your finger takes across the keyboard. As you glide your finger across the keyboard to spell out the word, suggestions for that word appear above the top line of keys. When you stop moving your finger, the word you've written is automatically recognised and inserted into your message.

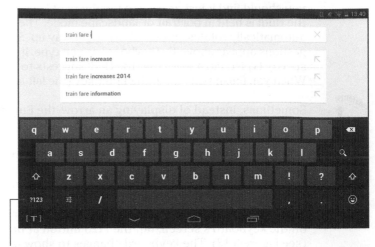

Switch to numeric keyboard

Figure 3-13: Tap the ?123 button on the alphabetical keyboard to get to the numeric keyboard.

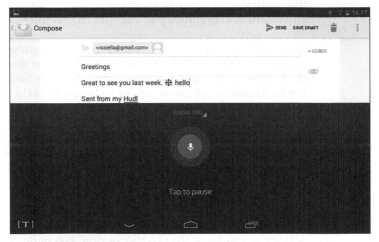

Figure 3-14: You can dictate messages by tapping the microphone icon to start the voice-recognition tool on the Hudl.

# Setting Up the Hudl for a Child to Use

It's important to set up your Hudl so that each family member can use it. The best first step is to secure your own account with a passcode that kicks in whenever the screen is locked, and then set up separate child accounts. Your passcode ensures that other people can't read (and reply to) your emails just by tapping the Email icon, for example. Chapter 2 describes how to use the screen lock feature.

In the case of younger family members, it's likely that you'll want to limit some of the websites they can go to and some of the tasks they can launch. You probably don't want your five-year-old to be able to buy items within a supposedly free game or to rent a film without your knowledge. You don't want to let them see what's on your part of the Hudl, either, so they can't watch films you've downloaded or browse through your photos.

An advantage of controlling access to your Hudl is that it stops anyone from taking items off it without your knowledge. If someone plugs your Hudl into a computer when the screen is locked, the Hudl won't appear as a connected device and they won't be able to see anything on your Hudl to copy.

A screen-lock passcode won't apply to anything stored on a memory card installed on your Hudl, though. Nothing stops another person from removing the micro-SD card and copying its contents, so if there's something important on the micro-SD card, copy it to the Hudl and then delete it from the card.

## Creating a separate account for a child (or other user)

One of the most effective ways to make your Hudl child-safe is to give your children their own accounts, with limitations on the apps they can use and the websites they can access.

This approach won't work if your child can simply choose to use your account instead, so make sure you've applied a screen lock to your account first.

To set up a new account on your Hudl, follow these steps:

1. **Drag the Quick Settings menu down from the top right of the screen, and tap Settings.**

2. **Scroll down the Settings page, and tap Users⇨Add User.**

   The next screen lists you as the owner (see Figure 3-15), and a pop-up message warns that the new user has to go through the Hudl setup process.

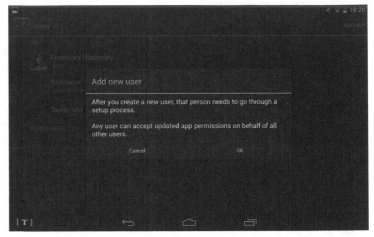

**Figure 3-15:** You can set up a separate user account for another family member to use in a matter of minutes.

3. **Tap OK.**

4. **On the next screen, tap Set Up Now to confirm that the new user account can be set up immediately.**

   The lock screen appears, with an added icon for the new user account (see Figure 3-16).

14:43

MON, DECEMBER 30

Charging, 31%

Figure 3-16: When there's more than one user account on the Hudl, separate login accounts appear onscreen. Make sure you add a screen-lock password to each one.

5. **There's no password on the account yet, so swipe to unlock the screen.**

   You see a message informing the new user that he or she will be able to use the Hudl in their own right, but the owner can delete apps and other items from it.

6. **Add the new user's Google or other email account details, if you want, and register his Tesco Clubcard account, if he has one.**

   An advantage of giving the new user a free Clubcard account is that he can enjoy free music and TV without needing to use your Google account.

   When the email details have been added, the All Done message appears, showing that the Hudl is now set up for the new user. Your child can now use your Hudl but won't be able to use your account.

## Limiting access to adult content

You can apply a variety of settings to limit a user's access to websites, movies, games and apps that include content not suitable for children. The next section of this chapter describes how to block apps with content inappropriate for younger users. Chapter 7 details how to restrict adult content in YouTube and BBC iPlayer, and Chapter 10 explains how to check content ratings on games.

# Downloading Apps from the Google Play Store

The Google Play Store offers thousands of apps to customise your Hudl and extend what it can do. You'd be hard-pressed to think of something that there *isn't* an app for.

To download apps from the store, you need to have a Google account (see Chapter 2) and add payment information to it so that you can pay for any apps that cost money and for any music, films or books you decide to buy. Many items are offered for free, but for paid-for items you will need to provide your card details.

To download an app from the Google Play Store, follow these steps:

1. **Tap the Google Play icon (refer to Figure 3-6) to go to the Google Play Store site.**

2. **Tap Apps.**

3. **Type the name of an app or its function into the box next to the magnifying glass at the top of the screen, or browse the apps by category.**

   Tap Categories at the top left to see a list of app types (see Figure 3-17), or tap one of the options running along the top of the screen to see the most popular free, paid-for or new apps.

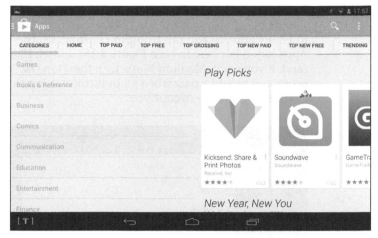

Figure 3-17: You can search for an app by category, as well as view the most popular paid-for and free apps.

4. **To get more information about an app, tap its icon.**

   Each app in the store has star ratings and reviews.

5. **When you've chosen an app, tap Install. If it's a paid-for app, you need to confirm the purchase by tapping Buy.**

6. **Provide your payment details, if you haven't already.**

   Make sure you're somewhere private when you add your bank information to your Google account. Then, as soon as you've associated your bank card with your Google account on your Hudl, make sure that you add a screen-lock password (see 'Setting a screen-lock password' in Chapter 2). If you don't, anyone who picks up your Hudl will be free to tap the Google Play icon and buy anything they want to.

7. **Once the app has downloaded, you see options to Open or Uninstall it. Tap Open to launch it immediately.**

If you prefer not to see adult content on your Hudl, or if you're setting up an account for a child to use, you can block apps aimed at older users.

To do this, tap the vertical menu bar at the top right of the Google Play Store screen, and choose Settings. Scroll down to User Controls, and tap Content Filtering. On the Allow Apps Rated For screen (see Figure 3-18), untick High Maturity (and, if you want, Medium Maturity); then tap OK. You'll be prompted to add a password so that this setting can't be changed by anyone except you.

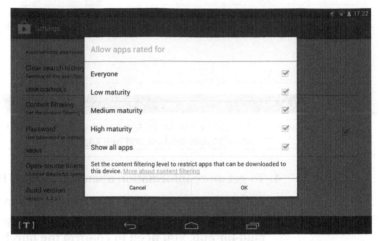

Figure 3-18: You can instantly block adult content being found in the Google Play Store by changing the Content Filtering options.

If you want to find out what each level of maturity rating involves, tap the More About Content Filtering link at the bottom.

# 4

# Connecting the Hudl

*A*s you see time and again in this book, your Hudl is at its most useful and most impressive when it's used in conjunction with something else, whether that's the Internet, your home network or a service that works alongside it.

Your Hudl can use the Internet wherever a Wi-Fi signal is available. Wi-Fi is a way of connecting to the Internet without cables. It's perfect for a portable device such as the Hudl, as it means you can get online almost anywhere. It means you can use the web all around your home if you have a Wi-Fi network online, or just look for a sign saying Wi-Fi is available when you're out and about. Sometimes, you need to pay to use the web connection, but thousands of places let you connect to the web wirelessly for free.

I explain how to find free Wi-Fi connections later in this chapter, in the section 'Connecting to a Wi-Fi Hotspot'. So long as you've got a Wi-Fi connection, you can check your email, get directions and browse the web. You can also listen to as much music as you want to and even watch films by streaming them over the Internet.

Your Hudl has lots of other connection options, though. If you connect to your computer or home network, you can copy items to your Hudl or transfer photos and music to your computer so that they're safely backed up.

# Connecting to a Wi-Fi Network

Wi-Fi is a wireless technology that lets you use the Internet and connect to other technology products without having to physically attach your Hudl to them. To find a new Wi-Fi connection to log on to, tap and hold the top-right corner of the Hudl's screen. Continue holding that corner, and drag about halfway down the screen. As you drag downwards, a grid menu should appear, like the one shown in Figure 4-1. This menu is the Quick Settings menu. You'll find it useful when you want to check the status of your Hudl's battery and connections and to change other settings.

Figure 4-1: Use the Quick Settings menu to check your Hudl's Wi-Fi connection status.

The fan-like icon on the left of the middle row in the Quick Settings menu is the one that relates to Wi-Fi. If the Wi-Fi icon shows any blue, you're already connected to a Wi-Fi network. (Chapter 2 discusses how to set up your Hudl for Wi-Fi access.) The name of the network you're connected to appears below the Wi-Fi icon. If only one or two bars are blue, the Wi-Fi signal is quite poor. In this case, it might be worth looking for a stronger signal. If the whole fan is blue, the signal is as strong as it can be.

If the Wi-Fi icon is blank, as in Figure 4-2, the Wi-Fi radio is switched off. It's switched off automatically if you put the Hudl in Aeroplane Mode, for example. (You see whether your Hudl is in Aeroplane Mode on the same screen.)

Figure 4-2: You won't be able to get online if the Hudl's Wi-Fi radio is switched off, as it is here.

Just tap the Wi-Fi icon to go to the Wi-Fi settings screen. Tap the word *Off* at the top to turn on the Wi-Fi radio. The Hudl scans for wireless networks in the area and then lists them. Tap a wireless network to connect to it.

If the Hudl lists lots of Wi-Fi networks, make sure you're connecting to the right one. Your neighbours may be upset if you connect to their Wi-Fi network without asking first! You can usually tell which connection is yours, because the wireless network bears the name of the broadband provider you use (unless you've changed it previously).

If you're at home and trying to connect to your own network, it's fine to connect to the network shown, even if it doesn't ask you for a password. If you see a padlock on the Wi-Fi icon, the connection is password-protected. The Hudl's keyboard pops up, along with a box where you can type the password (see Figure 4-3). Passwords are case-sensitive so make sure you take notice of which letters need to be uppercase and which are lowercase when typing in the password.

As you see in Figure 4-3, some acronyms above the Password field describe the type of security the network uses. As long as the Security field says *WPA* or *WPA2*, it's very secure. Tap Connect after you type the password. After a couple of seconds, the word *Connected* should appear below the network's name. Tap the Home button at the bottom of the screen to go back to the Hudl's Home screen.

WiFidelity 5GHz

| | |
|---|---|
| Signal strength | Good |
| Security | WPA/WPA2 PSK |
| Password | | |

Show password

Cancel

Figure 4-3: To join a Wi-Fi network, type its network password and then tap Connect.

To turn off the Hudl's Wi-Fi connection, go to the Quick Settings menu and tap the Wi-Fi connection on the left of the middle row. (You see the connection name rather than the word 'Wi-Fi'.) You now see the available Wi-Fi connections list again. Tap the On button at the top right to switch off the Wi-Fi. The next time you want to connect to Wi-Fi, just tap the same button again and the Wi-Fi will turn on. If a Wi-Fi network you used before is available, the Hudl will automatically connect to this network.

# What is Wi-Fi?

*Wi-Fi* stands for *wireless fidelity*. Wi-Fi uses a type of radio wave to transmit and receive information. Whenever the Wi-Fi on your Hudl is switched on, it broadcasts its presence to other wireless devices in the area. Devices that have Wi-Fi do the same, which is how they are able to find and connect to one another.

# Connecting to a Wi-Fi Hotspot

You may have heard of a hotspot — somewhere that you can get online wirelessly and use the Internet. Hotspots are tailor-made for use with your Hudl. Lots of places offer Wi-Fi these days, some for free and some not.

## Finding a hotspot

If you've got your Hudl with you, and you want to get online, look out for a sign in the window of a shop or other business. Often, this sign has a distinctive black-and-white Wi-Fi logo like the one shown in Figure 4-4. This symbol is the official logo of the Wi-Fi Alliance, the organisation that makes sure that products that have a wireless chip work with one another properly.

Source: Wi-Fi Alliance

Figure 4-4: Look for the black and white Wi-Fi logo. It indicates somewhere that you can get online on your Hudl.

Many places offer free Wi-Fi access as long as you buy something. Just ask the person serving you for the Wi-Fi details when you're paying for your coffee or cake. You need to know the name of the network as well as the password to connect to the network.

You can instantly see whether your Hudl is connected to a Wi-Fi network by looking for a tiny version of the small blue Wi-Fi icon discussed earlier in this chapter (refer to Figure 4-1). This icon appears next to the time and the battery indicator at the top right of the screen. The signal strength is shown, too. If you find it hard to work how many bars are shown, just drag down on this part of the screen to see a larger status screen.

## Staying safe with Wi-Fi

Because your Hudl constantly transmits its location when Wi-Fi is switched on, it's very easy for other devices that also have Wi-Fi to find it. Hackers often lurk in places where Wi-Fi users are likely to be — coffee shops and tourist locations are popular choices — and set up an unsecured wireless network in the hope that people will log on to it. Because there's no password to remember and the connection doesn't cost anything, there's a fair chance that people will use it.

A free Wi-Fi connection may really be a trap, however. While you're busy checking your email, looking at Facebook or consulting your bank balance, a hacker may be installing software on your tablet that tells him or her what you type on it, such as your credit card number or the password for your online banking service. It isn't wise to shop online at a public location just in case someone peeks over your shoulder and makes a note of your credit card number and security code, but it's definitely risky to do so via an unsecured Wi-Fi connection.

It's much better to play it safe and stump up the pound or so that it costs to buy web access, or to wait until you can find a free hotspot that is secure. If you can find only unsecured Wi-Fi for free, use it only to go online and find the nearest free Wi-Fi that *is* secure. You can use the free WiFi Finder app (https://play.google.com/store) or the hotspot-locating website iPass (www.ipass.com).

# Connecting to Other Devices with Wi-Fi Direct

Wi-Fi Direct allows you to connect to another device without first having to connect to a wireless network. This feature can be useful when you need to copy something between devices but don't have a cable to physically connect the devices or a way to share the item via email. It's also really useful if you've got a broadband connection that your laptop uses for web access but don't have a Wi-Fi router. Connecting your Hudl to your laptop with Wi-Fi Direct allows you to use the laptop's web connection. In this situation, the laptop creates a Wi-Fi hotspot just for your Hudl to use.

# What is Wi-Fi Direct?

Wi-Fi Direct is a fairly new technology that's available only on phones, tablets and a limited number of laptops that were made in the past three years. If you're trying to connect to an Android tablet or phone using Wi-Fi Direct, the Android device must run Android 4.0 or later. Windows works with Wi-Fi Direct, too.

The easiest way to find out which of your other devices work with Wi-Fi Direct is to try to connect to them. In this section, you give it a try.

 You can't connect to an iPhone or iPad with Wi-Fi Direct because Apple uses a different, incompatible type of wireless connection technology. You can use Bluetooth to connect your Hudl to an Apple device or a laptop in order to transfer items between them.

## *Using Wi-Fi Direct*

To use Wi-Fi Direct, follow these steps:

1. **Pull down the Quick Settings menu from the top right of the screen (refer to 'Connecting to a Wi-Fi Network' earlier in this chapter).**

2. **Tap the Wi-Fi icon to go to the wireless networks menu.**

3. **Tap the vertical bar at the top right to display a menu of options (see Figure 4-5).**

Figure 4-5: Switch on Wi-Fi Direct in the menu bar at the top right of the Wi-Fi Settings screen. You'll now be able to share photos and files with other devices that use Wi-Fi Direct.

### 4. Tap Wi-Fi Direct.

Your Hudl scans the airwaves, looking for devices that it can connect to (see Figure 4-6). If it doesn't find any devices, there aren't any other phones, tablets or laptops in range that have Wi-Fi Direct, or their Wi-Fi radios aren't switched on. If it does find one or more devices, they'll appear in the list.

Figure 4-6: Searching for a Wi-Fi Direct device to connect to. The Hudl is listed as an Android device.

5. **To send something to another device using Wi-Fi Direct, tap the item you want to share, tap the Share icon at the top right of the screen, and then tap Wi-Fi Direct and the device you want to send it to.**

## Renaming your Hudl for easy ID

When the Hudl searches for Wi-Fi Direct devices (see the preceding section), it lists itself as an Android device. You can rename your Hudl to make it easier to identify, however, such as when you want to connect to a Wi-Fi network or another device.

To rename your Hudl, tap the Rename Device option at the far right of the screen (refer to Figure 4-6 earlier in this chapter). The current name is highlighted in the Rename Device box that appears (see Figure 4-7). Type a new name, and tap OK to confirm the change.

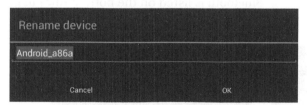

Figure 4-7: Renaming your Hudl makes it easier to identify when you're connecting it to other devices.

# Using Your Hudl's Bluetooth Connection

Bluetooth is another sort of wireless connection, used to connect devices that are in fairly close proximity. You can connect devices that are up to 30 feet away from each other, but ideally, they'll be much closer. Unlike Wi-Fi, Bluetooth isn't intended to pass through walls, so you may not be able to use it to connect your Hudl to a laptop in another room. Bluetooth works best when the two devices are in sight of each other and nothing is blocking them.

You can use Bluetooth to share the web connection of a 3G or 4G-enabled phone. You'll then be able to get online on your Hudl even if you don't have access to a Wi-Fi hotspot. I look at how to get online this way in 'Sharing a web connection with your phone' later in this chapter.

Bluetooth is also really useful for connecting to items such as speakers or a keyboard. You make the connection from the Hudl and usually only need to push a button on the other device to confirm the connection. For details, see 'Connecting a keyboard or speaker' later in this chapter.

## *Starting and using Bluetooth*

To switch on and start using Bluetooth, follow these steps:

1. **Tap and drag down the Quick Settings menu from the top right.**

   Bluetooth is listed on the bottom row but greyed out, as shown in Figure 4-8.

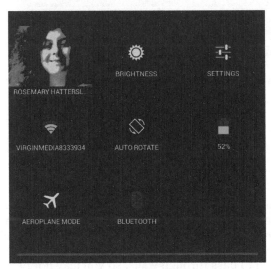

Figure 4-8: You need to switch on Bluetooth so it can find devices to connect to.

2. **Tap the Bluetooth icon to go to the Bluetooth settings menu.**

3. **Tap the word *Off* at the top to change it to *On*.**

   Bluetooth automatically lists your Hudl as *Hudl,* so you don't need to change its name so that other devices can easily recognise it (see 'Renaming your Hudl for easy ID' earlier in this chapter).

4. **Tap Scan for Devices.**

   It takes about 10 or 20 seconds for the scan to locate Bluetooth devices that are in range. Then these devices appear in an Available Devices list (see Figure 4-9).

   If you're trying to connect to a phone or tablet that's in range of your Hudl but doesn't appear in the list, Bluetooth is probably switched off on that device. Find the Settings menu on the device (on an Android phone, a square blue icon with slider bars on it, the same as the Settings app on the Hudl). Scroll down to Bluetooth, and tap On to make it active. Now go back to your Hudl and tap Scan for Devices again. This time, the device should appear in the Available Devices list.

**Figure 4-9:** Bluetooth devices that are in range appear in the Available Devices list on your Hudl.

5. **Tap the name of the device that you want to connect to.**

   If you're trying to use Bluetooth to connect to a phone, tablet or laptop, you need to be able to see its screen as well as the Hudl's.

   A string of numbers (known as a *passkey*) appears on your Hudl's screen and on the screen of the device you're trying to connect to.

6. **Confirm that the passkeys listed on your Hudl and the other device match, and then tap OK or Pair on both devices (see Figure 4-10).**

   The devices are paired and listed in a Paired Devices list (see Figure 4-11).

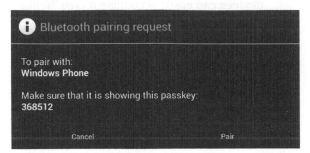

**ⓘ** Bluetooth pairing request

To pair with:
**Windows Phone**

Make sure that it is showing this passkey:
**368512**

Cancel                              Pair

Figure 4-10: Make sure that the passkeys are the same on the two devices you're trying to connect.

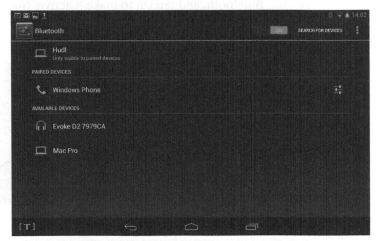

Figure 4-11: When your Hudl is connected to another device, it appears in the Paired Devices list and has a 'paired' icon next to it.

When devices are connected, you can send items between them. You could share a photo by using Bluetooth, for example. To do this, tap the Gallery app on the Hudl's Home screen, tap the photo you want to share, tap the branch (share) icon, tap See All. Bluetooth will now appear as a sharing option (see Figure 4-12) and then tap Bluetooth to send the photo to the paired device. I look at how to take and view photos on your Hudl in Chapter 6.

Share photo
via Bluetooth

Figure 4-12: It's easy to share photos with friends by using Bluetooth.

To disconnect from another device your Hudl is paired with using Bluetooth, go to the Quick Settings menu and tap Bluetooth; then tap the On button at the top right of the Bluetooth device screen to change its status to Off. Tap the On/Off button again to make Bluetooth active again. If the device your Hudl was paired with before is still in range and no passcode was required to pair them originally, they will pair again automatically.

## Connecting a keyboard or speaker

Connecting via Bluetooth to a device that doesn't have a screen on which to check a passkey works slightly differently. You still need to go to the Bluetooth settings menu and tap Scan for Devices (see 'Starting and using Bluetooth' earlier in this chapter), but when the speaker or keyboard appears in the list, just tap its name to connect to it. The word *Connected* appears below it. Now you can use the connected device as though it were attached to your Hudl.

If this technique doesn't work, check whether the device you're trying to connect to has a button other than the power button. If you find such a button, press it and then tap the device's name in the Bluetooth list on the Hudl. The devices should pair.

You may need to select Bluetooth as the output option when you're playing music over a Bluetooth speaker.

## Sharing a web connection with your phone

If you've got a smartphone that has 3G or 4G web access, you can use Bluetooth or Wi-Fi to connect your Hudl to it and then make use of its web connection on your Hudl — a procedure known as *tethering*. Only some phones and tablets allow you to do this, however.

To find out whether your phone lets you tether a laptop or tablet so it can get online, check the terms of your mobile phone contract. Some mobile phone networks let you add tethering if you pay an add-on charge to do so. If you've got a pay-as-you-go phone (in other words, you have to top up the airtime credit when it gets low), you probably won't be able to use it for tethering.

If your phone contract does allow you to use the phone for tethering and you want to use Bluetooth, turn on Bluetooth on both the Hudl and the phone, activate the phone's Settings and Hotspot menus and pair the two devices as described in 'Starting and using Bluetooth' earlier in this chapter. To use Wi-Fi for tethering, select Portable Wi-Fi Hotspot as your tethering method in your phone's Tethering and Portable Hotspot menu.

# Connecting Your Hudl to a Computer

You have lots of ways to connect the Hudl to a computer:

✔ If you're using a laptop with Windows 7 or 8, you should be able to connect via both Bluetooth and Wi-Fi.

✔ You can physically connect to a Windows computer or laptop by using the Hudl's USB cable. With this connection, you'll be able to quickly share a large number of photos, music and videos. This option is great if you've already got a lot of music and photos on your computer.

To connect this way, just plug the micro-USB end of the cable into your Hudl and the other end into a USB port on your computer. After a few seconds, the word *Hudl* should appear in the Devices list below the icon for your computer. Click this word. Make sure that you have internal storage selected (as shown in Figure 4-13). Then drag across any music, photos and videos you'd like to be able to play or watch on your Hudl.

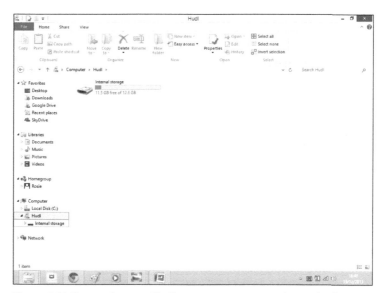

Figure 4-13: Connecting your Hudl to your computer can be as simple as connecting it via USB.

⮞ To connect your Hudl to an Apple computer, you can also use the USB cable. However, you will need to install Android File Transfer for Mac software (www.android. com/filetransfer) on your Apple computer. Once that program is installed, you can drag and drop files and folders into the File Transfer folder. Click Transfer when you're ready to copy everything to the Hudl.

See Chapter 8 for more about the music formats that your Hudl can recognise and other ways of getting songs onto it.

When you've started taking photos and recording videos on your Hudl or saving other types of files on it, you'll be able to copy them to your computer for safekeeping, too. Depending on the settings you choose for your Hudl, these types of files may be backed up to Google's servers automatically. You see at how to back up your Hudl using Google Drive in Chapter 11.

To copy an item across from your Hudl, plug your Hudl into your computer. The computer recognises whether you have new items on it that haven't yet transferred and offers to copy them (see Figure 4-14). Photos are automatically copied to a new Pictures folder on the computer. Just overwrite the folder name (to which the current date is automatically assigned) with a more memorable name and then click OK.

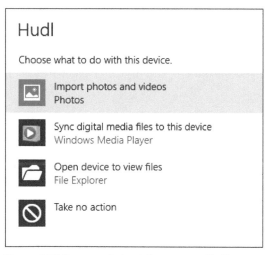

Figure 4-14: To copy photos taken on your Hudl to your computer, just plug the Hudl into the computer and choose the Import option.

# Connecting Your Hudl to an HDTV

One really great way to use your Hudl is to connect it to your high-definition TV so you can watch films, play a slideshow of photos stored on the Hudl or play Android games on a much larger screen. To do this, you need an HDMI (high-definition multimedia interface) cable with a micro-HDMI connector at one end. This cable isn't supplied with the Hudl but you can buy a two-metre micro-HDMI to HDMI cable from the Hudl accessories page of Tesco Direct.

Before you buy an HDMI cable, first check that your TV has an HDMI port that will accept the HDMI connection.

When you've connected your Hudl to your TV, switch the input source on your TV to HDMI. Your TV shows whatever is on the Hudl's screen. You don't need to change anything on your Hudl to make it play on the TV. Because the HDMI cable carries sound as well as HD video, you'll also be able to watch videos stored on your Hudl by connecting it to your HDTV.

If you'd like a slideshow to appear on the TV, tap the Gallery app on the Hudl's Home screen and then tap the folder containing the photos you'd like to look at. Tap the vertical bar at the top right; then tap Slideshow. The photos should play in turn.

Don't forget to bear in mind that anyone who's in the room will be able to see what's on the screen too, so check that your photos and videos are suitable for family consumption!

# 5
# Staying in Touch

. . . . . . . . . . . . . . . . . . . . . . . . . . . . . . . . . . . . . . . . . .

## In This Chapter

▶ Using Gmail to contact people

▶ Using other email services on your Hudl

▶ Socialising with Facebook

▶ Making video calls with Skype

. . . . . . . . . . . . . . . . . . . . . . . . . . . . . . . . . . . . . . . . . .

*Y*our Hudl offers lots of ways to keep in touch with friends and family and to keep up to date with what's going on in the world. Chapter 2 establishes one way of keeping in touch, as you create a Gmail account on your Hudl when you first get everything set up.

You can also use your Hudl with any other email programs, however, and view all your messages on it. If you prefer to switch to Gmail, I show you the easy way to send all your emails there.

You'll probably find yourself using the Internet more and more now you've got a Hudl, because it's so easy to get online and see what's happening. If you've decided that it's time to dive into the world of social networks, I show you how to use Facebook on your Hudl.

You may prefer to chat to your friends rather than simply send them messages. In this chapter, I also show you how you can make free calls from your Hudl or even chat with friends face to face by using the Hudl's built-in cameras.

## Sending Emails from Gmail

I show you how to use a Gmail account to set up your Hudl in Chapter 2. If you already have a Google account, you probably have some contacts in your Gmail contacts list already.

If Gmail is new territory for you, this section shows you how to use it on your Hudl.

To launch Gmail, tap All Apps (the white circle with the dots in on the vertical menu); then locate the Gmail icon within the folder. The Gmail icon is a white envelope with a red *M* inside it (see Figure 5-1). The *M* is for *mail,* as in 'You've got mail'. When you tap it, your inbox opens, showing you a list of the new messages you've received together with the start of each message and its sender.

You can add Gmail to your Home screen by dragging it to the Home screen. The Home screen appears when you tap and hold your finger on the Gmail icon in the All Apps folder. Lift your finger off the screen to place the icon on the Home screen.

Gmail icon

Figure 5-1: Drag Gmail to your Home screen from the Apps list so it's easier to get to your emails.

If unread emails are waiting for you, a tiny envelope icon appears in the notifications menu at the top left of the Hudl's Home screen (see Chapter 3). You can drag this icon down to see how many messages you've received. It's more convenient, however, to simply use Notifications as an alert to new messages and events and to go to the Gmail app to see all your emails. Notifications about new messages appear at the top left of your screen. New emails are shown as tiny white envelopes.

# Opening and replying to an email

To read a message in your inbox, tap to open it. If the message is quite long, you may need to use a finger to scroll through it. If you rotate the Hudl through 90 degrees so that it's in portrait mode, the email message rotates automatically and goes into full-screen mode so you can see much more of it (see Figure 5-2).

**Figure 5-2:** Rotate your Hudl so it's in portrait mode, and you'll be able to see far more of your email message at once.

To reply to an email, follow these steps:

1. **Tap the arrow pointing to the left in the bar at the top of the message.**

   The word *Reply* and your email address appear at the top left of the screen. Below, in the To field, you see the name of the person who emailed you.

2. **Tap the area next to the flashing cursor, and type your response.**

3. **Check for any underlined words, which indicate that something may be misspelt, and correct the spelling of any words that need it.**

4. **Tap Send.**

   When you've replied to a message, your Google profile photo appears next to the profile photo of the person you just responded to. If you don't have a Google profile photo, Gmail instead uses a coloured tile with the person's initial to help make it easier to see who's who in your email inbox (see Figure 5-3).

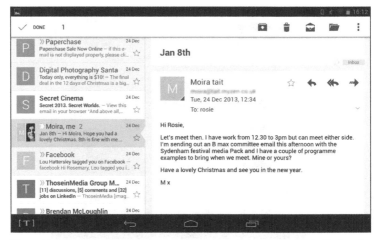

**Figure 5-3:** Gmail colour-codes messages to make them easier to find and shows profile photos if they've been added to someone's Google account.

# Creating and sending a new email

Here's how to create and send a new message:

1. **Tap to open Gmail; then tap the envelope with the +
   sign next to it at the top right of the screen
   (see Figure 5-4).**

   Your email address appears at the top of the screen,
   and on the next line, you see a cursor blinking in the
   To field.

Create new email

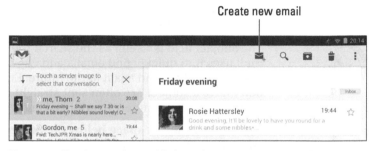

Figure 5-4: Tap the envelope with the + sign to start a new email.

2. **Tap the To field to type the email address of the
   person you want to send a message to.**

   If you've received any emails from this person already,
   Gmail should recognise the name and offer to complete the email address for you.

   If you've never corresponded with this person before
   (or not from this email account), you need to know
   his or her email address. If the person you're trying
   to email is someone you know, you can simply ask to
   swap email addresses.

    If you're trying to contact somebody at a business,
   try looking on the company's website, as staff email
   addresses may be listed there.

If you can't find the person's email address right now or haven't got time to finish writing your email, tap Save Draft and come back to the message later. (If the Save Draft option isn't already shown onscreen, you can locate it in the menu at the top right.) Gmail usually saves drafts for you anyway, but if the message is important, it's worth tapping Save Draft just to be on the safe side.

3. **Tap the next line down, which is the Subject field, and enter the subject of your email.**

   It's polite to add a subject to your emails, as it lets the recipient know what you're contacting her about. If you simply want to say hello, it's fine to type 'Hello from *[your name]*' in the Subject field. If you forget to include a subject line with your message, you may get a prompt reminding you to add one.

   The Subject field is useful as the search tool on your Hudl uses it to quickly find emails and conversations you may want to read again in the future. Emails that don't have a subject are often sent straight to the spam folder or are simply overlooked and go unread.

4. **Tap the large blank space below the Subject field, and type your message.**

5. **When you finish writing your email message, tap Send.**

   If you left a blank where the email address should be, a message states *You must include at least one recipient.* Type an email address and then tap Send.

## Getting addresses right

If you're telling someone your email address, make sure you provide the following things:

✓ **Structure**: You need to state what appears after the @ ('at') sign as well as the words or letters in front of it. Be sure to include the .co.uk, .com or similar portion of the address.

✓ **Spelling**: You may need to spell out your email address letter by letter so the email is definitely delivered to you. If something isn't spelled right, the email won't be delivered.

# Sending photos by email

You can also send photos to friends in an email. Here's how:

1. **Complete Steps 1-3 of 'Creating and sending a new email,' earlier in this chapter.**

2. **Tap the picture-frame icon at the end of the Subject field to add an attachment.**

3. **Tap Gallery or Photos to see the photos stored on your Hudl.**

4. **Tap the photo you want to email to your friend.**

   The photo you select appears at the bottom of the draft email message (see Figure 5-5).

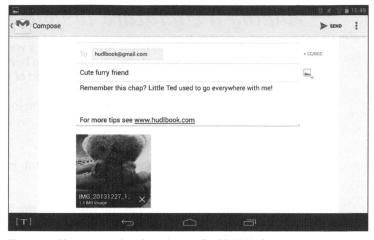

Figure 5-5: You can send a photo by email with just a few taps.

5. **Complete your email as usual and then tap Send.**

   When your friend receives the email, it will have a paperclip icon with it, which means that the message has an attachment. To see your photo, your friend just needs to click or tap this attachment.

## Sending one email to several people

If you want to send the same message to more than one person at the same time, tap a blank area of the To field and then type another email address. All the people to whom you send the message see your message — and also one another's email addresses.

To send the same message to several people without revealing everyone's email addresses, enter their addresses in the Bcc field. (*Bcc* stands for *blind carbon copy*.) This way, the same message goes to all the people in the list without showing who else is getting the message.

## Adding a signature to your email

If you want your friends to know how to contact you other than by email, or to tell them that you're emailing on behalf of an organisation, you can add a signature to the end of your emails.

You can add a signature to your emails by changing the settings in your Google account online at mail.google.com or in your Email or Gmail app on your Hudl.

To change the message via your Google account, follow these steps:

1. **Tap the Google icon at the top left of the Hudl's screen and type** Gmail account **to go to the sign-in-page for your Gmail account.**

2. **Tap the cog icon on the right side of the screen and tap Settings and scroll down to Signature.**

3. **If No Signature is selected, tap the button beneath this option.**

4. **In the box that appears, type the signature message that you want to appear at the end of every message you send (see Figure 5-6). Your Twitter name, phone number or Skype account name are useful options here (I cover Skype video calls later in this chapter).**

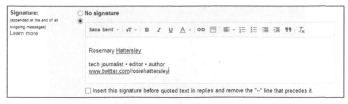

Figure 5-6: Add a new signature for your emails.

5. If you want to, change the font and type style for your signature using the options above the text box.

6. When you're happy with your signature tap Save Changes.

Now when you go back to the Gmail app, your signature is added to all the new emails you compose.

# Adding More Email Accounts to Your Hudl

You aren't limited to using Gmail on your Hudl; you can easily add other email accounts. To do so, follow these steps:

1. Pull down the Quick Settings menu at the top right, and tap Settings.

2. In the Accounts section of the Settings screen, tap Add Account.

3. On the next screen, shown in Figure 5-7, tap Email. Ignore the Google and Tesco options as these just show you which email address is associated with their respective services.

4. On the next screen, type your name and the email address and password you use with that account; then tap Next.

The computer that looks after the email service's login details checks your information. As long as your details and password match, you'll be able to use this email account on your Hudl from now on.

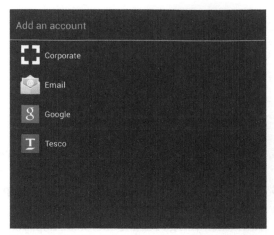

Figure 5-7: Tap Email to add a new email account to your Hudl.

If you want to use your Hudl to access your work email, you probably need to get permission and the domain name of the server from whoever manages your office network. (It's probably best to get that person to set everything up for you too.)

# Being Social with Facebook

Facebook (www.facebook.com) can be brilliant for keeping up with friends and rediscovering people you haven't seen for years. Download the Android version of the Facebook app to use Facebook on your Hudl. (Chapter 3 explains how to find and download apps from the Google Play Store.)

If you already have a Facebook account, you're ready to go. If you don't have an account, you'll need to set one up at Facebook.com. Although you can login to a Facebook account through the Facebook app, you need to create the account online first. Just fill in the requested information on the Sign Up form at Facebook.com to get started (see Figure 5-8).

**Figure 5-8:** You can download the Facebook app to your Hudl and create a Facebook account in just a few minutes.

You're required to type your name and email address and add your date of birth. Facebook won't allow you to create an account if your date of birth indicates you're younger than 13. Also, you must choose and type a password. (Don't use the same one for your email and other accounts.) Then tap Sign Up to create the account.

Before you can go any further, you need to confirm your account setup. Go to your email account and open the message from Facebook headed 'Just one more step to get started on Facebook'. Then tap Confirm Your Account, or note down the five-digit code in the bottom right of the email, type this code in the box labelled Enter Confirmation Code in Facebook and then tap Confirm. You see a confirmation message and an option to install the Facebook app on your Hudl. If you've already installed the app, just tap Open on the next screen.

## Applying privacy settings

It's best to limit who can see what you post on Facebook to Friends Only. To do so, tap Privacy Shortcuts and then tap the arrow next to Who Can See My Stuff? (see Figure 5-9). By default, this option is set to Public. Tap this entry to change this option. Tap Friends or Acquaintances (which includes family members and friends).

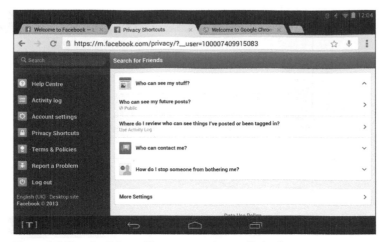

Figure 5-9: Use the Privacy Shortcuts settings to limit who can see your Facebook posts.

Now you're asked to upload a photo of yourself (or to take a new one) that can be used as your Facebook profile photo. Facebook won't let you set up your account without a photo.

## Finding friends

Facebook works by connecting friends and encouraging them to share ideas and chat with one another. To join in, you need to ask someone to be your friend. Tap the menu at the top left of the Facebook page, tap Find Friends and type a name in the Name or Email search box. Facebook tries to help, listing people with matching names who live in the same town or country and are approximately the same age as you. People who don't have anything in common with items on your Facebook profile are listed farther down.

Photos can make all the difference, so if you're looking for someone who has a common name, you can exclude people who don't look at all like the person you're after. Look carefully, though: Some people post old photos of themselves or post pictures of their kids instead, so there can be red herrings.

When you find someone you know, tap their name, and you should see their profile page, which shows as much or as little information as they've decided to make publicly visible. Tap Add Friend to send a friend request.

## *Sharing messages and comments*

When you've made friends with someone on Facebook, you'll be able to see each other's photos, exchange messages via Facebook email, chat when you're both online and share interesting web links.

To comment on friends' photos, links and status updates, just tap Like (as I have in Figure 5-10), or tap Comment and type a message about the item your friend posted. You can also tag your friends in photos that include them. To do this, tap the photo and then type your friends' name to tag them.

**Figure 5-10:** When you add a photo or status update on Facebook, your friends can like or comment on it.

## Setting up a child's Facebook account

You must be at least 13 years old to have a Facebook account. You can't set up and manage a Facebook account on your child's behalf, so if your child has a Facebook account, you'll have to be vigilant about the settings in use. Make sure the privacy and sharing settings applied to that account don't let the whole world see what your child is up to. In addition, I strongly recommend that you read the advice on Facebook's Family Safety Centre page (https://www.facebook.com/help/safety?rdrhc), shown in Figure 5-11. As well as offering useful privacy tips, this page provides help and contacts if you think that your child is being bullied through Facebook or another website.

Figure 5-11: Parents should consult Facebook's Family Safety Centre about privacy and sharing settings for younger users.

If someone is annoying you on Facebook, you can block him. To do this, tap the menu at the top left of the Facebook screen and then tap Blocking; you see a screen like the one shown in Figure 5-12. Type the person's name or email address and then tap Block. You won't be bothered anymore.

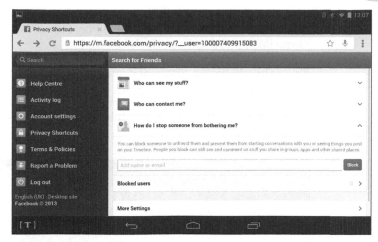

**Figure 5-12:** You can easily block anyone on Facebook whom you find annoying.

 You can find lots of information about setting up and using Facebook at www.dummies.com/how-to/internet/Blogging-Social-Networking/Facebook.html. Tap or click a link in the Topics list to find out about using Facebook safely, connecting to friends and posting photos and videos, among other topics.

# Chatting to Friends with Skype

Video calls can be a wonderful way to get closer to someone you can't easily see in person, such as a relative or dear friend who lives overseas. The microphone and front camera on the Hudl make it ideal for having video chats with friends. Better yet, you can make calls for free by using Wi-Fi (if the person on the other end also has Skype or a similar program). You just need an email address and a free app that stores your contacts and dials the person you want to contact. You don't need a real phone at all.

You can use lots of services to make free phone calls and video calls over Wi-Fi. The best-known service is Skype (www.skype.com), so I cover it in this section.

You can download the Android app from www.skype.com or download Skype from the Google Play Store. You need the Skype IM app rather than the Wi-Fi one.

If you already have a Skype account, you can begin using Skype on your Hudl straight away. If not, you need to set up a Skype account. As you can see in Figure 5-13, if you have a Microsoft account, you can use this username and password with Skype.

Figure 5-13: You can use any Microsoft account to log in to Skype and make phone and video calls over Wi-Fi.

Logging in with an existing account is handy, as you'll be able to make calls via Skype to anyone in your contacts list who also has a Skype or Windows Messenger account.

If you don't have a Microsoft account, tap Create Account at the bottom of the Skype sign-in screen and then create a Skype account, following the prompts on the screen.

Find out more about how to use Skype at www.dummies.com/how-to/content/the-essentials-of-communicating-with-skype.html.

# Finding and adding Skype contacts

Next, you need to find people to call. To add new people, tap the face icon at the top of the screen and then tap Add People (see Figure 5-14). Next, search by name or email address for friends and family members who also have Skype accounts. When your friend's name appears, tap Add Contact. Your friend is sent a message saying you'd like to add them as a contact.

Figure 5-14: Tap Add People to start a search for friends who also use Skype.

# Making a Skype call

To make a Skype call, follow these steps:

1. **Tap the telephone icon next to the word *Skype* at the top of the screen.**

2. **Tap People⇨Skype. Your Skype contacts list will appear.**

### 3. Do one of the following:

- To make a voice-only call, tap the telephone icon.

- To make a video call, tap the video-camera icon. This icon launches the Hudl's front camera (see Figure 5-15).

If the person you're calling is available to chat, he'll tap the green phone icon in Skype to accept your call. His webcam starts working, and you'll be able to see him after a few moments. Give him a wave to say hello.

Figure 5-15: Tap the video-camera icon to make a video call with Skype.

 Be sure to position your Hudl so that the camera is pointing approximately at your forehead. It's best to check in advance that the webcam has you properly in shot and that it isn't pointing at your chin (not very flattering) or aimed so far upwards that your smiling face can't be seen.

 Consider whether you're going to have a quick chat with a friend and will be fine holding the Hudl for the duration of the call, or whether you're calling someone for a lengthier catch-up. If you're expecting to chat for a while, you'll find it easiest to prop up the Hudl. If you become a regular Wi-Fi video correspondent, it's worth buying a stand to keep the Hudl upright. If you're a bookworm you'll probably also appreciate not having to hold the tablet for hours at a time while reading books on your Hudl.

# Calling landline and mobile phones

You can use your Hudl to call people whose phone numbers you know, but you can't do this for free. To make calls to landline and mobile phone numbers, you need to set up a paid-for Skype account and add some credit to it. This is worth doing, because the calls are usually much cheaper, particularly if you're calling someone who lives in another country. It's also really useful if you're travelling overseas and need to call family members back home. Just pop your Hudl in your bag, and you've got a money-saving way to stay in touch.

Call prices vary, depending on which country you're calling, but you can find a list at www.skype.com/en/rates. International calls can cost next to nothing.

# Improving Skype call quality

The Wi-Fi icon in the top right of the Hudl's screen shows how strong the Wi-Fi connection is. The better the Wi-Fi connection, the better the video and phone call quality will be. If you got only one or two bars of Wi-Fi, you may find that the call drops out or the audio is so poor that it's hard to make out what the other person is saying. If possible, move somewhere where the Wi-Fi signal is stronger.

# 6

# Taking Photographs

. . . . . . . . . . . . . . . . . . . . . . . . . . . . . . . . . . . . . . . . . . . . . .

## *In This Chapter*

▷ Taking photos and videos on your Hudl

▷ Viewing your photos in the Gallery

▷ Editing your photos and videos

▷ Sharing your photos with friends

▷ Backing up your photos to Google Drive or your computer

. . . . . . . . . . . . . . . . . . . . . . . . . . . . . . . . . . . . . . . . . . . . . .

*O*ne of the most fantastic things about the Hudl is how well it displays photos. Photos that you take with the Hudl's own camera and those you import from elsewhere are all stored in one place, where you can easily call them up.

The Hudl's lovely 7-inch display has a resolution of 1,440x900-pixels, which is just right for viewing a selection of photos side by side or looking at one in detail. Better yet, you don't need to use a separate app to open your photos or to edit or share them.

The Hudl has a 3MP (megapixel) camera built into its rear and a 2MP camera on the front. Both cameras can be used to record video as well as taking photos. You can even use them to hold video chats with friends over the Internet.

You don't need to worry about overloading your Hudl with photos, either. A full 16GB of storage space is built in, which means there's ample space to store the photos that you take on the Hudl, and to copy lots of others to the device too. You can also insert a micro-SD card (a tiny storage card of the type found in smartphones) into a slot on the side of the Hudl and view or copy photos that are stored on it. Cards of up to 32GB capacity can be read. Any useful information about each photo, such as when and where it was taken, is copied to your Hudl too, which makes it really easy to organise your collection and find the photo you want to look at.

You aren't limited to viewing your own photos on your Hudl. You can also open and view photos that friends send you by email before choosing whether you want to save them to the Hudl's memory. You can also view photos that are part of your own online archive without having to copy them to the Hudl first. I cover this in 'Backing up your photos to Google Drive' later in this chapter.

In fact, you can view as many photos as you like on the Internet, on photo-sharing websites such as Flickr (www. flickr.com) and Photobucket (www.photobucket.com), and on sites you use to keep in touch with friends, such as Facebook (www.facebook.com).

The next few pages walk you through how to take photos using the Hudl's own camera and present several options for getting photos you've already taken onto your Hudl.

# Taking Photos with Your Hudl

You can switch between the Hudl's two cameras at any time, but the one on the rear is more commonly used for taking photos of things around you and the one on the front is often used as a video camera or to take 'selfies' (photos of yourself). The camera on the back can capture more detail than the front camera, although both cameras can take photos and record video. Chapter 5 covers how to set up a video conversation with a friend using Skype.

To take a photo on your Hudl, press the Home button and then tap the camera icon that appears in the top right corner of the screen. The camera lens is on the back of the Hudl. If you're holding the Hudl in two hands, and it's in landscape mode, the lens is at the top left. If you're holding the Hudl in portrait mode, the lens is at the top right (and the power and volume buttons are at the bottom).

Hold the Hudl as steady as you can, and frame your subject. If you like, you can tap an area of the photo to indicate that it's the main subject (as shown in Figure 6-1). The camera focuses on this area and ensures that it's really sharp while you finalise framing the shot. When you're ready, tap the blue shutter button to take the photo. Unless you've turned down the Hudl's volume, a click confirms that the photo has been taken. To take another photo, just frame your shot and tap the blue shutter button again.

Figure 6-1: Tap the main subject of your photo to focus on it. Tap the blue shutter button to take the shot.

Your photos are stored in the Hudl's Gallery, which you can access within the camera app by swiping across the screen from right to left.

## Taking successful photos

The scene and editing modes on the Hudl are useful for achieving particular effects, but there's no substitute for setting up a photo well in the first place.

As with any other camera, the most important element is light. If you have plenty of natural light, you're far more likely to get a good photo. Indoor shots and ones taken over a long distance come out less well because the camera has to work harder to distinguish objects. If there's no way to get more natural light into the shot by repositioning yourself, there may be a way to add more light by reflecting some back into the shot or by using artificial light. If these options aren't available, you need to use the Hudl's camera settings (discussed in the following section) to improve the light balance. You look at how to edit photos on your Hudl after you've taken them in 'Editing Photos on Your Hudl', later in this chapter.

You'll quickly discover that taking photos on your Hudl can be a bit unwieldy. We just aren't used to using a tablet to take photos, so the process doesn't feel very natural. It can be tricky to hold the camera steady while you're taking a shot. If you accidentally move, any blurring that occurs will be exaggerated in a close-up photo.

A better way to take close-up shots is to hold the Hudl steady a foot or so from the object you want to photograph. Take care not to have other objects immediately adjacent to your object. Take the photo as usual by tapping the object to focus on it and then tapping the blue shutter button. This technique should result in a sharper shot. After the photo has been saved to your Hudl's Gallery, you can use the editing tools to crop it so that the detail you wanted to photograph in the first place becomes much more prominent.

Using a prop to steady your Hudl as you take photos with it helps ensure that your photos are sharper.

## Getting more from your Hudl's camera

Some great camera options on your Hudl can help you refine your photo skills even more.

### Turning off the dark (or the light)

To control how light or dark a photo will be, follow these steps:

1. **Tap the Home button and then tap the camera icon.**

2. **Frame the image you want to shoot in your camera display.**

3. **Tap the big empty circle that appears above the blue shutter button.**

   You see the camera settings (with the Hudl in portrait orientation) in Figure 6-2.

Switch front/back cameras

Light source settings
Image size and storage settings
Change light levels

Take a photo/video
Still/video camera toggle

Figure 6-2: The camera settings give you lots of control of your photos.

4. **Tap the +/– icon to display the light-adjustment menu.**

5. **To make the camera brighten the image, tap +1, +2 or +3; if the image is too light, tap –1, –2 or –3; to go back to the original setting, tap 0.**

The Hudl's display changes according to the setting you choose and shows how light or dark the photo will be if you take it with that setting.

6. **To take the photo, tap the blue shutter button on the right.**

Don't worry too much if the photo comes out too dark or light; it's very easy to change it later with the Hudl's photo editing tools (see 'Editing Photos on Your Hudl' later in this chapter).

*Setting the scene*

Another useful camera option is the scene type. To access the Scene Mode option, tap and hold the A/W icon on the viewer. This long press brings up five scene options, as you see in Figure 6-3). Here you can switch from auto/white balance (the default option) to cloudy, sunny, party (the cracker icon) and artificial light.

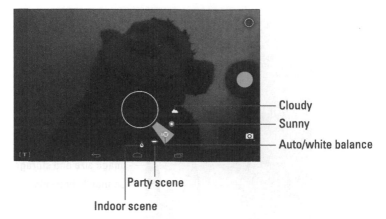

Figure 6-3: You'll get better photos if you select the correct type of lighting for your scene.

# Taking pictures of your Hudl's screen

In addition to using your Hudl's built-in cameras to take pictures of what you see through the camera lenses, you can take shots of whatever's on the Hudl's screen. This feature may be handy if you want to save a copy of a web page to refer to later — when you find a recipe you like, for example, or when you want to photograph the transaction confirmation for something you buy so you can use the photo as a receipt. Or you may simply have got a great score in a game you've been playing on your Hudl and want to save the screen showing that score so you can brag to your friends!

To photograph what's on your Hudl's screen, press the power button and the volume down buttons on the side of the tablet at the same time.

The process is a bit fiddly, so you'll have to be patient, as making it work can take several attempts and takes a second or two to work. Most times, you'll accidentally change the volume instead.

When you've got your Hudl to take a screen shot, you should hear a click (the same one that sounds when you take a photo with the cameras). The screen flashes and your screen image appears with a white border around it. The screen shot is saved to the Gallery along with all your other photos.

# Creating panorama photos

One of my favourite things to do on the Hudl is take panorama photos. The Hudl's design lends itself perfectly to this process; it's easy to hold the device steady in two hands and then simply sweep slowly from left to right to take the shot.

To create a panorama, follow these steps:

1. **Tap the Camera icon and then tap the white camera at the bottom right of the screen.**

   Three icons are displayed; the concave icon on the left is the Panorama option.

2. **Tap the Panorama icon.**

3. **Frame the image you want the panorama to start with.**

4. **Tap the blue shutter button to start recording.**

5. **Turn slowly in an arc from left to right.**

   Try to keep the Hudl at a constant height as you turn. Also, don't move too fast; if you do, the image will come out blurred. You'll also get onscreen warnings: a red frame around the image and a Too Fast message.

   As the recording progresses, the panorama icon that appears below the picture slowly fills, showing how much of the scene has been recorded (see Figure 6-4).

Figure 6-4: Shooting a panorama.

6. **The Hudl automatically stops recording and splices together the images for the panorama for you.**

The Hudl automatically saves your panorama scene to the Gallery.

 Before you create a panoramic shot, it's best to check that you can smoothly and steadily move from left to right to fit the whole scene in. It's also handy to have a quick practice so you can check for unexpected objects, such as pillars you hadn't noticed, and for people who might walk into the shot.

# Recording Video on Your Hudl

You can record video on your Hudl really easily. Just tap the Camera app on the Home screen and then tap the camera icon that appears at the bottom right. To select video recording mode, tap the video camera icon (the middle one of the three options shown). Now hold up your Hudl, frame your video and tap the large red Record button when you want to start filming. Tap this button again to finish recording. You'll be able to see how much footage you've recorded, as there's a timer in the top left.

 One fun fact about the Hudl's video camera is that it can take still photos even while it's recording a video. All you have to do to take a photo while in video-recording mode is tap the screen.

 Be careful not to tap too hard when you tap the screen to take a photo while recording video. If you do, the tablet may move, resulting in a blurred photo or shaky video footage.

The video footage that you shoot on your Hudl appears in the Camera folder in the Gallery. Video clips have a white play button over the image. Tap this button to play your video. (You look at how to play videos you download or copy from other sources to your Hudl in Chapter 7.)

# Viewing Photos on Your Hudl

You have lots of options for viewing photos on your Hudl. First, however, you need to know where photos are stored on it. All photos taken on your Hudl are saved to the Gallery app. To get there, tap the Home button and then tap the Gallery icon — the picture-frame icon in the top right of the screen.

The 8 photos taken on your Hudl most recently will appear in the Gallery app in *Grid View* (see Figure 6-5). To see more photos, slide your finger to the left or right. To view a single photo in detail, tap it to make it appear full-screen; tap it again to return to Grid View or pinch and zoom to make it bigger or smaller. You can switch from Grid View to Filmstrip View in any Gallery folder by tapping the arrow next to the Gallery icon at the top left and tapping Filmstrip View.

Grid view                                          Overflow menu bar

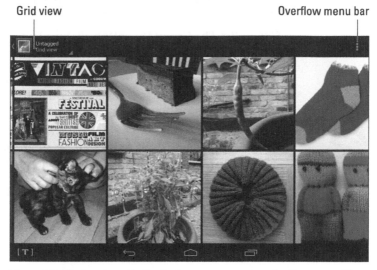

**Figure 6-5:** Photos stored in the Gallery app are automatically arranged into folders you can flick through in either Grid View or Filmstrip View.

When you start saving photos from emails, downloading them from Facebook or Flickr or taking screenshots on your Hudl, new folders will be added automatically in the Gallery to keep your photos organised. Photos taken on the Hudl will appear in a Camera folder.

You can go back to the Grid View at any time by tapping the Camera folder in the Gallery (which stores only photos taken on the Hudl's camera).

## Displaying your photos

To view your photos in various ways, tap the Overflow menu bar (the vertical bar icon) at the top right of the Gallery screen and make a choice from the resulting menu:

✔ **Slideshow:** All the photos in the same folder play in sequence. To change folders, tap the Gallery icon at the top left to show a grid of folders and then tap the one you want.

✔ **Group By:** The Group By option allows you to sort photos by Location, Time (when the photos were taken), People and Tags. Time and Location information are added to photos automatically, but photos are only sorted by People and Tags if you've added this information to the photos before they were saved on your Hudl.

If you plan to copy lots of photos from other sources and store them on your Hudl, it's best to name the folders and add any tags you want to include before adding the files to your Hudl. Your Hudl can organise those photos by tag only if you add tag information to them before you copy them to your Hudl.

## Adding a profile picture

You can add a profile picture for any person in your Contacts list. (For details, see Chapter 2.) To do so, follow these steps:

1. **Tap the photo you want to use.**

2. **Tap the Overflow menu bar in the top right of the screen.**

3. **Choose Set Picture As⇨Contact⇨Find Contacts to bring up the onscreen keyboard.**

4. **Type the name of the person in the photo.**

You can use this technique to make any photo in your Hudl Gallery your own profile picture.

## Setting a photo as your Hudl's background image

You can use a photo you really like as the background image on your Hudl, as long as that photo appears in the Hudl's Gallery.

To use a photo as a background image (also known as *wallpaper*), follow these steps:

1. **Tap the Gallery icon.**

2. **Tap the photo you want to use.**

3. **Tap the Overflow menu bar in the top right of the screen and choose Set Picture As⇨Wallpaper.**

   You can also change wallpapers by holding your finger on an unused part of the Hudl's screen until the Wallpaper menu appears and then choosing a photo you want to use.

 If you've got lots of apps and other items strewn all over the Hudl's screen, it's probably best to choose a photo that doesn't have too much distracting detail; otherwise, you'll find it hard to see what all those apps are.

## Editing Photos on Your Hudl

Your Hudl has lots of great editing options for you to explore. You can add colour filters, change the contrast levels, crop shots and add arty effects.

### Adding effects

To apply an effect to a photo, follow these steps:

1. **Tap the Gallery icon.**

2. **Tap the photo you want to edit.**

3. **Tap the Photo Edit icon (the concentric-circles) in the bottom left of the screen.**

   Small thumbnail images of your photo appear below the original shot (see Figure 6-6).

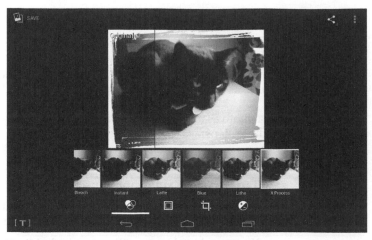

Figure 6-6: Instantly preview photo effects in this screen.

4. **Hold your finger on one of the thumbnail images and then move your finger left and right to see the different effects that are available.**

5. **Tap one of these effects to apply it to your photo.**

6. **Do one of the following:**

   - To save the image with the effect applied, tap Save in the top left of the screen.

   - To leave the image unchanged, select the None effect from the left end of the thumbnail strip, or tap the back arrow at the bottom of the screen to return to the original image.

To quickly compare the effect you're applying to a photo with the original version, hold your finger on the image and then slowly swipe up or down. A split-screen view shows the original photo and the effect you're overlaying.

## Adjusting photo settings

You can edit your photos in other ways. To do so, follow these steps:

1. **Tap the Gallery icon.**

2. **Tap the photo you want to edit.**

3. **Tap the Photo Edit icon and then swipe your finger over to the icon with the + and – minus signs (refer to Figure 6-4 earlier in this chapter).**

   The resulting menu lists options that let you adjust 11 elements of your photo and is the most powerful editing tool on your Hudl.

4. **Select the option you want to use, and make the desired changes in your photo.**

All the options except Autocolour and Curves have sliders that you can use to adjust how much you want to change your photo. If you select Sharpness and drag its slider to the left, for example, you can make the image a little less sharp; drag the slider to the right, and you make the image a lot crisper. Tap Save to apply the changes or undo the last change by tapping the back arrow at the bottom of the screen.

## Undoing your changes

If, having made several changes to your photo, you decide that you don't like the result, you can get rid of the last set of changes you made by tapping the Overflow menu in the top right of the screen and then choosing one of the following options:

- **Undo:** Tap Undo to get rid of your most recent change.

- **Reset:** Tap Reset to get rid of all your changes.

- **Show History:** If you liked some of the changes you applied, tap Show History to see a list of the edits you made and the order in which you made them.

## Storing tags with your photos

Your Hudl records where a photo was taken (so you can easily retrieve the shot later based on this information), as long as you have Location Access switched on. Unless you change your Location Access settings from the default, your Hudl should save location information with each photo when it's taken. (This information includes the street name but not the house number.) To see the location information, tap a photo to view it full-size, and then tap the Overflow menu bar in the top right. Tap Details to see when and where the photo was taken, as well as the camera settings used.

## Exploring fun photo and video apps

You can use lots of great photo and video apps to add particular effects to your images. To find links to some of the best photo apps for your Hudl, tap the Getting Started widget and then follow the links to PicsArt, Flickr and other great apps.

 If you use an app to take photos on your Hudl instead of using the device's cameras, location information is stored with those photos as long as you've allowed the app access to it. Location information is calculated via GPS (Global Positioning System) and Wi-Fi.

You can turn location access on and off in the Settings menu by following these steps:

1. **Tap the area in the top right of the screen where the time is displayed.**

2. **Drag downwards and release your finger when a grid of menu options appears.**

3. **Tap Settings; then scroll down to the Personal section and tap Location Access.**

4. **Toggle the Access to My Location setting on and off, or individually tick and untick the GPS Satellites and Wi-Fi & Mobile Network Location options.**

5. **Tap the back arrow or the Home button at the bottom of the screen after you've made your changes.**

# Editing Video on Your Hudl

You don't have as many options for editing videos on your Hudl as you have for editing photos. Two options are definitely worth getting to know, however, and I cover them both in the following sections.

# Viewing video details

The Details menu shows you important information about your video clip. To view it, follow these steps:

1. **Tap the Gallery icon.**

2. **Tap the Camera folder in the Albums menu to bring up Grid View.**

   The Albums folder is automatically created when you add photos from different sources.

3. **Tap the white play button on a video clip to display it full-screen.**

4. **Tap anywhere within the image except the play button and then tap the Overflow menu bar in the top right.**

5. **Choose Details from the resulting menu.**

   You see the time and date when the video was shot, as well as the clip's duration, its file size and where it's stored. A 20-second clip takes up roughly 20MB of storage.

# Editing video length

If you recorded an overly long clip, or if only some of the footage contains any action, you may prefer to chop out the boring bits where nothing's happening. As you may realise from consulting the Details screen (refer to 'Viewing video details' earlier in this chapter), video files are very large, so it makes sense to delete clips you don't want or to reduce their length so you've always got plenty of space on your Hudl for other things.

To make a video clip shorter, follow these steps:

1. **Tap the Overflow menu bar.**

2. **Choose Trim from the resulting menu.**

   Your video plays so that you can see the whole thing and identify where to make the clip stop or start.

3. **As the video plays, drag the blue markers at the bottom of the screen to make the video start from or stop at these points (see Figure 6-7).**

You can adjust a marker's location by holding your finger on it and sliding it to the left or right. Tap the button in the middle of the screen to replay the scene.

Figure 6-7: Drag the markers along the video timeline to trim the beginning and end.

4. **When you're happy with the length and content of your video clip, tap Save in the top left.**

A new, shorter version of your video is saved to the Gallery. If you want to, you can delete the original version of the video by selecting it, tapping the Overflow menu bar and then choosing Delete.

# Sharing Your Work with Others

Your Hudl makes it easy to share your photos and videos with family members and friends. The tricky part is deciding which sharing option to choose.

To share, follow these steps:

1. **Tap the photo or video you want to share.**

2. **Tap the Share icon (denoted by three joined dots) in the top right of the screen.**

   You see several options, including Hangouts, Picasa and Keep, all of which are services that Google offers. You don't have to use them, however.

3. **To see more options, tap See All.**

   The options list expands to show Bluetooth, Google+, Gmail and Drive (see Figure 6-8).

Figure 6-8: Tap See All to get an extensive list of ways to share photos from your Hudl.

4. **Tap the service you want to use to share the photo.**

One of the easiest sharing options to use is Gmail (see Chapter 5), which lets you send a photo by email straight from the Gallery. Tap the Gmail icon, tap the blank space next to the magnifying glass and type your friend's email address. If that person is in your Gmail Contacts list, his email address may appear in the suggestions list; otherwise, type his complete email address. Add a subject to the email and/or a message in the email itself and then tap Send.

## Viewing and sharing non-Hudl photos

Photos that you take on your Hudl by using an app rather than the Hudl's own camera won't show up in the Gallery automatically. To view these photos, you need to open the app that they were taken in. Depending on the app, you may be able to share these photos by using the options within the app. If you really want to make these photos appear in the Hudl's Gallery, try emailing them to your Gmail address and then saving them from Gmail to the Gallery.

Another fun way to share a photo is to use Hangouts. Hangouts are great ways to share items with several friends at the same time so everyone can comment on them. You can use Google+ to share something publicly straight from the Gallery, too. Tap the photo you want to share, tap the Share icon and then tap Google+ in the list that appears.

You can also share your photos on social media sites such as Facebook (www.facebook.com) and Twitter (www.twitter.com), as I explain in Chapter 5. You can also share them via Bluetooth (see Chapter 4).

# Storing Your Photos and Videos in Google Drive

Google Drive is a free app that you can use to store all sorts of items. It's especially handy for storing all your photos and videos so you can access them from your laptop or home computer as well as from your Hudl. You can either view them online through the Google Drive app or make items in your Google Drive available offline, in which case they will be saved to your Hudl.

The option to save single items to Google Drive is built into the Hudl. To use it, follow these steps:

1. **Tap the photo you want to upload to Google Drive.**

2. **Tap the Share icon and choose Drive from the resulting menu.**

3. **(Optional) To rename your photo before you upload it to your Google Drive account, tap the image name and then overwrite it.**

4. **When you're ready to upload the photo, tap OK.**

You can view your stored photos and videos by logging in to your Google account on your computer and clicking the Drive option. I look at Google Drive in more detail in Chapter 11.

# Copying Photos and Videos to Your Computer

The simplest way to copy lots of photos or videos from your Hudl to your computer is to connect the devices via the Hudl's USB cable. On most PCs, your computer displays a message asking what you'd like it to do when you plug in your Hudl. Click this message and then click the Import Photos and Videos option. Photos from your Gallery are copied to a folder in the computer's Pictures library that's labelled with the current date.

On a Mac, the Hudl will appear in the Devices list, but only if you have Android File Transfer installed (`www.android.com/filetransfer`). For both Mac and PC, the Hudl will only appear at all if the Hudl's screen is unlocked.

# 7

# Watching TV and Films

*I*t's no accident that the Hudl's screen is just the right proportions for playing TV programmes and films. Its high-definition1440x900-pixel display also means that any video you play is shown off in lavish detail. The great news is that you can watch a fantastic array of films, TV programmes and online video on your Hudl. As I show you in Chapter 4, you can also make anything that you can play on your Hudl screen play on your high-definition television (HDTV) screen by connecting them using a micro-HDMI to HDMI cable.

What's even better is that you can enjoy plenty of video and TV on your Hudl for free. Just create a Clubcard TV account, and you'll be able to take your pick from some classic TV programmes and films. Many of the titles in the Clubcard TV library are suitable for kids, so make this your first port of call when you need to entertain them.

You'll also find lots of free kids' TV programmes on YouTube — I show you where to look — and BBC iPlayer is bound to become a firm favourite with the whole family.

Finally, I look at renting films and TV episodes 'on demand' through blinkbox movies and the Google Play Store. You certainly won't be short of viewing options!

# Making the Most of YouTube

YouTube (www.youtube.com) is a vast online video library that you can delve into as much as you want to. A link in the Favourites bar on your Hudl — the red Play button — takes you straight to YouTube. When YouTube first opens, you see lots of 'popular' content, most of which has been uploaded (shared on the YouTube website) by teenagers.

If you don't want bad language or raunchy videos to appear, tap the menu at the top right; then tap Settings⇨Search and tap to change SafeSearch filtering from Don't Filter to Strict. This process should save a few red faces when you're using YouTube on your Hudl with your children.

To find a particular video or topic on YouTube, just type it in the search box at the top of the screen, or tap the menu bar at the top left to reveal entertainment categories. Tap an item to start playing it. When the video starts playing, the playback controls appear at the bottom of the video. These controls fade from view after a couple of seconds. However, they reappear if you tap the screen. Tap the square icon at the bottom right of the playback controls to make the video play full-screen. To stop a YouTube video playing, just swipe it off the edge of the screen.

I recommend you create a YouTube account because you'll then be shown the sort of videos and programmes you really enjoy and get notifications about new episodes. Lots of amateur and semi-professional TV channels exist only on YouTube, and it's worth subscribing to any that interest you. To subscribe, just tap the Subscribe button on the right side of the screen (see Figure 7-1).

Subscribe

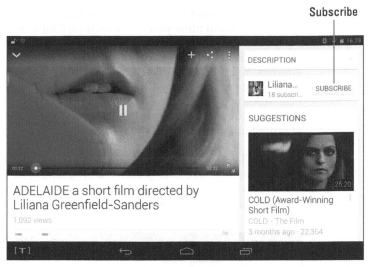

ADELAIDE a short film directed by
Liliana Greenfield-Sanders

**Figure 7-1:** It's easy to search for or subscribe to YouTube video channels.

You can find plenty of free films to watch on YouTube, though you won't find the latest blockbusters because of licensing and copyright issues. You need to buy or rent these titles from the Google Play Store or blinkbox movies instead, as I show you later in this chapter. You'll find plenty of classic Westerns, comedies and action movies from the 1990s and earlier, however.

Use Google to search for lists of films you can watch on YouTube. Film buffs pride themselves on coming up with lists of the 'best' films you can watch, so save their lists and use them as a guide to what you should be able to watch for free.

# Watching Free Programmes on Clubcard TV

Clubcard TV is just what it sounds like: a TV service for anyone who has a Tesco Clubcard. If you don't have a Clubcard, apply for one at www.tesco.com/clubcard. When you've been issued with a Clubcard membership number, just set up an account (using your email address) and create a password for it.

As soon as you sign in, you see thumbnails of the TV programmes and films you can watch on Clubcard TV (see Figure 7-2). A G next to a programme shows that it's suitable for most viewers, but it may go over the heads of very young viewers. You can check the suitability of a programme by consulting the parental guidance page at www.clubcardtv.com/about/parentalguidance. If you want to, you can apply a PIN code to stop programmes and films that are rated anything other than U (for universal) being watched.

Clubcard TV programmes are streamed over Wi-Fi and can't be downloaded. A red strip above a programme or film's title warns you that it won't be available through Clubcard TV much longer, so you may want to prioritise watching it.

Figure 7-2: Clubcard TV is a free TV and film library for Tesco Clubcard members.

 Because the Hudl is designed for all ages to enjoy, it doesn't have a very loud speaker, as loud volumes can damage young ears. To get the most enjoyment from watching TV and films on your Hudl, I recommend adding a Bluetooth speaker such as the HDMX JAM, shown in Figure 7-3 and available from Tesco Direct (see Chapter 12). This way, you'll be able to crank up the volume and enjoy the dialogue and sound effects to the full.

Figure 7-3: Using a Bluetooth speaker can really enhance your movie-viewing experience.

# Tuning in to BBC iPlayer

I'm sure you've heard of BBC iPlayer — a catch-up TV service you can use to watch BBC programmes for a few days or weeks after they're first broadcast. The free BBC iPlayer app for Android makes it easy to search through what's on offer and also manages iPlayer downloads for you. Downloads are handy because you can watch them when you don't have a Wi-Fi connection for your Hudl (when you're on the train, for example).

To get started, download BBC iPlayer from the Google Play Store. The option to watch live TV has recently been added to iPlayer too. If you choose to watch live BBC TV (which I cover later in this chapter), you're prompted to install the BBC Media Player app.

As you see in Figure 7-4, BBC iPlayer lists Most Popular and Featured programmes, and offers a Channels view. You can scroll through any of these views to find something you like or tap the magnifying glass on the menu bar at the top to search for a programme.

Figure 7-4: Take your pick from a constantly updated selection of programmes on iPlayer.

When you find a programme you want to watch, just tap it to start viewing it immediately. Tap the screen to pause it. The *S* to the right of the progress bar denotes subtitles; tap it to add captioning to the programme. If you stop watching a programme, it automatically resumes from where you left off when you return to it.

## Setting parental controls

If you want to, you can impose a Parental Controls lock on BBC iPlayer so that your children can't watch programmes that weren't intended for their age group. Here's how:

1. **Tap Settings⇨Parental Guidance Lock.**

2. **Choose a four-digit PIN, and tap Continue.**

3. **Choose a secret question to answer in the event that you forget your PIN.**

4. **Tap Activate to apply the lock.**

# Downloading programmes to watch later

Downloads buy you more time to watch something, so if you want to watch something that's going to be on iPlayer for only a few more days, it's best to download it as soon as possible. Tap Download beneath the programme's description to start downloading it to your Hudl. As you see in Figure 7-5, after you download a programme you have 30 days to start watching it and a week to complete doing so. After the 30 days are up, the download won't play any longer.

**Figure 7-5:** You can download programmes to your Hudl to watch at your own pace.

# Watching live BBC programmes

Live TV viewing is a new addition to BBC iPlayer. To see what's currently being broadcast, follow these steps:

1. **Choose Watch Live from the top-right menu. To watch live broadcasts you need to install the BBC Media Player. Tap Install to go to the Google Play Store to install it.**

   A list of BBC programmes currently on air appears.

2. **Tap the programme you want to watch.**

A message warns you that you must have a TV licence to watch live TV. As long as you have a TV licence for your home, you're allowed to watch live TV broadcasts on your Hudl too.

3. **Tap Watch Now.**

---

# Watch even more catch-up TV

The BBC iPlayer isn't your only TV-viewing option. Here are a few others:

✔ ITV, Channel 4 and Channel Five each have their own apps that you can use to watch TV shows on demand. Just search for and download the apps from the Google Play Store.

✔ If you've got Sky satellite TV, you can use the SkyGo app for free to watch both live TV and programmes on demand. Note that you need to type 'SkyGo' with no space as the search term. You just need your Sky ID and password. If you're not a Sky customer, you can pay to access its content to watch via the app.

✔ Another good option is Crackle (see the figure below). This Sony-backed app offers a strong selection of free TV programmes and films; you just need to put up with intermittent adverts. Crackle can't be customised, but you can apply parental controls, and you can save films you want to watch later to your watch list.

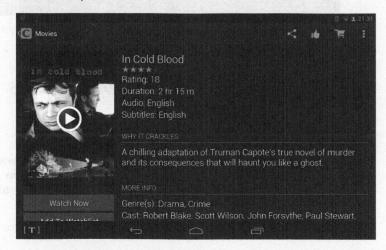

---

# Renting and Buying Movies

You have lots of ways to get movies you can watch on your Hudl. blinkbox movies is a great, flexible option as you only pay per item. Another option is to buy a film from the Google Play Store and download it to your Hudl. Subscription services are only worth getting if you watch lots of films.

## Getting content from blinkbox movies

blinkbox movies is a great film and TV rental service that doesn't commit you to a monthly subscription. You just need a free blinkbox account. You have the choice of renting films or buying them. Most films cost £3.49 to rent or £9.99 to buy, but regular offers let you rent films for 99p each. TV episodes typically cost £1.89 each.

blinkbox movies is already installed on your Hudl. You can open it by going into All Apps from the Favourites bar, by accessing it from the blinkbox widget pre-installed on the Home screen, or by tapping the [T] at the bottom left of the screen and tapping blinkbox movies in the menu at the top left.

Films and TV have separate lists. To change between libraries, tap Movies and the option to switch to the TV library will appear (see Figure 7-6). TV and movie listings are organised by Latest, Featured, Top Rated and Best Selling and, of course, there's a search option. blinkbox movies regularly features exclusives, so it's worth checking for these or looking out for blinkbox emails about them.

When you've found something you want to watch, tap it to begin the purchase process. Swipe the screen upwards to see whether the film or TV programme is available for rental as well as to buy. If you're using blinkbox movies for the first time, tap Pay with New Card and provide your bank details. Your information is securely stored so you can make instant purchases in the future.

Select from movies or TV programmes

Figure 7-6: blinkbox movies has an impressive selection of TV programmes and films to choose from.

Anything you buy appears in your blinkbox library. Just tap the person icon in the top right to go to it.

Another option is to pay by voucher. If you have a blinkbox card, tap this option and then type in the voucher number. You'll be able to start watching the programme or film as soon as you tap Confirm and the payment is authorised. You can buy blinkbox vouchers and gift cards at any Tesco store or through Tesco Direct.

If you decide that you want to bookmark something and come back to it later (see Figure 7-7), you can tap Watch Later. This feature is handy as you don't have to pay up front and risk not getting round to watching it; the film or programme of interest will be waiting for you in your Watch Later folder. You can view this folder by going into your account.

Watch later

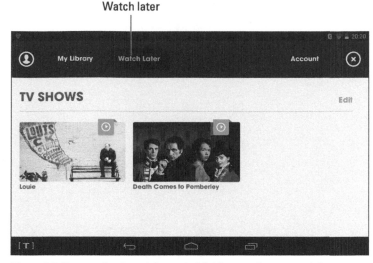

Figure 7-7: You can bookmark items in blinkbox movies to watch later.

# Getting content from the Google Play Store

To buy video content from Google, simply tap the Play Store button and search for the title you're after in the Movies & TV section.

You'll find good deals on box sets and TV series at Google Play Movies. As with other content you get from Google, you'll find a category search list at the top left, including a section for family film and TV. Purchases appear in My Movies & TV even farther to the left.

Google Play Movies gives you the option of HD (high-definition) and SD (standard-definition) versions of films and TV programmes. The prices vary too, of course. The HD series of *The Gruffalo,* for example, costs £6.99, whereas the SD version is only £4.99.

# 8

# Listening to Music

*T*here are lots of ways to enjoy music on your Hudl, with or without headphones plugged in. As long as the album or track you want to listen to is in a supported digital format — MP3 is the most common type — you'll be able to play it on your Hudl. Your Hudl can also play WAV, OGG and Flac music files.

You can store music on the Hudl itself and play songs through the Play Music app or listen to songs that are stored on your computer (or somewhere else on your home network), saving you even having to copy them to your tablet.

You can also listen to songs online for free using blinkbox music. With blinkbox music, you can start listening to songs immediately rather than having to buy songs and download them to your Hudl to play them from there. Listening online is known as *streaming,* as music is sent in a continuous stream of data to your Hudl quickly enough that it plays smoothly. Music played this way isn't stored on your Hudl, but you can often bookmark songs to come back to later.

Yet another option is to transfer the songs stored on a computer to your Hudl. I look at options for doing this later in this chapter.

You can use the Hudl's own speakers to listen to your music, or you can plug in headphones or use Bluetooth to connect to external speakers and use your Hudl as a mini entertainment centre. I look at useful accessories such as headphones and speakers in Chapter 14.

# Discover Free Music with blinkbox music

blinkbox music (www.blinkboxmusic.com) is a fantastic, free music-streaming app that comes with your Hudl. It lets you listen to free music 'stations' (similar to conventional radio stations), which are never-ending streams of music based around a common theme, mood, artist, song or genre. You can listen for as long as you want and, with a choice of thousands of stations, you're sure to find anything that you're after.

You can choose from a diverse range of pre-programmed stations (curated and constantly updated by blinkbox) or you can create your own customised stations by searching for any artist, song or genre you're in the mood for. blinkbox music will automatically create an endless stream of music similar to your choice. blinkbox music also offers a subscription service for £1-a-week that has no ads and lets you create your own playlists. You can have a total of 100 unique tracks at any point across all your playlists, and you can swap tracks in and out of your playlists whenever you like. A track that appears in multiple playlists is only counted once.

## Getting started with blinkbox music

To start using blinkbox music, follow these instructions:

1. **Swipe left to get to the screen with the blinkbox music widget; then tap Go.**

2. **Tap Sign Up for Free Music.**

3. **Sign in to your existing blinkbox account or create a new account by following the onscreen directions.**

   Several station options appear on the left side of the screen.

4. **Tap Explore Stations, and scroll down the list of stations until you find one you like the look of.**

5. **Tap the Play button on the right to start listening.**

   If you like what you hear, you can make the station a favourite by tapping the station's image and then tapping the star icon in the menu that appears. This station is saved, and you'll always be able to tune in to it again by tapping the Favourites option at the top of the screen.

## Searching for music

You can search for a band or song by tapping the Search for Music field in the top-right corner of the screen (see Figure 8-1). Type the artist or song name and then tap Go on the keyboard. blinkbox music finds or creates a station for you based on your chosen artist or song. You see a list of other artists included in the station to the right of the station's graphic. Tap the station's name to start playing it.

Search for music

Figure 8-1: You can search for your favourite band and listen to a station based on its songs.

## Saving a blinkbox music station or track

To save a station so you can listen to it whenever you want to, tap its image when it's playing and then tap Download This Station. From now on, when you tap the blinkbox icon at the top left, you'll find that station in the Downloaded Stations list.

It's a good idea to save stations this way, because although blinkbox music saves a history of the stations you listen to so that you can go back to them again later, it saves only the last five stations in its History list. Another good reason to save your stations is that blinkbox music can play anything that's in them even when it has no web connection to stream the music over. If you no longer have Wi-Fi access, blinkbox music automatically starts playing songs based on those in your list of stored stations. You can only save a station when you have an active Wi-Fi connection, however.

If a song that comes on isn't to your taste, tap the heart icon with the x in it, and in future, you won't hear this song again.

You can use any of the online music players and streaming services as much as you want to. However, unless you're able to download tracks and save them on your Hudl you'll only be able to play them when you're connected to the Internet via Wi-Fi.

## Customising blinkbox music

Below the Station options in blinkbox music is a Settings option. Tap it to see your existing account options, including whether stations are updated automatically. The Settings screen also lets you choose whether songs with explicit lyrics can be played (see Figure 8-2). It's a good idea to untick this option if your kids are likely to use blinkbox music.

Restrict songs with explicit lyrics

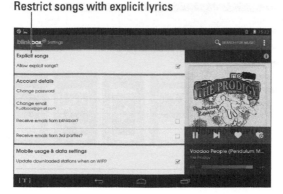

Figure 8-2: You can make blinkbox music child-friendly by suppressing songs with explicit lyrics.

# Listening to Music with Spotify

The simplest way to enjoy music on your Hudl is to listen to it online. Lots of music services let you listen to as much music as you like. One of the best-known examples is Spotify (www. spotify.com). You just need to have a Wi-Fi connection (see Chapter 4) so that the songs can be streamed to your Hudl. The songs play over the Internet, rather than being downloaded to your Hudl and playing from there.

You can create an account at the Spotify website and choose music to listen to there, but it's simpler to use the Spotify app (see Figure 8-3), which you can download from the Google Play Store.

Unlike most apps, Spotify insists on running in portrait view, so it's more like a book. An advantage of portrait mode is that you can scroll through playlists and artist lists efficiently because more information is displayed on each screen.

Figure 8-3: Although you can also use Spotify online, it's easier to install the free app on your Hudl.

# Signing up for Spotify

To get started using the Spotify app, follow these steps:

1. **Tap Sign Up and follow the onscreen instructions to create a Spotify account.**

If you've got a Facebook account, you can use your Facebook login details for Spotify. If you don't have a Facebook account, use the email address you created when you set up your Hudl (or another email address).

Make sure that you use a different password for Spotify than the one you use for your Google account (see Chapter 2), because if someone ever finds out the login details for a service or email account you use, the first thing they'll do is try the same password in all your other accounts. You'll be far better protected if you use a different password for each account.

2. **Provide your date of birth.**

   To do this, change the day, month and year by swiping your finger up and down the respective columns. The heading changes from the current date to Set Date. When the correct date is shown, tap Done. Now you can start using Spotify.

# Finding music to listen to

Spotify has millions of songs to choose from. You can listen to as many songs as you like, but you can't pick and choose specific songs if you use the free version of the Spotify app. (For details of the paid-for version, see the nearby sidebar 'How free and paid-for Spotify versions compare'.) Instead, songs are played in Shuffle Play mode, which is really a set of playlists based on a musical genre or mood (see Figure 8-4). When you tap to select a Shuffle Play category, you see a list of what's in the playlist you're about to hear. You also hear adverts periodically (which is what enables Spotify's makers to give you all this free music).

Top Lists is a good place to start. This category plays the 100 most popular indie, pop, alternative or rock tracks. Tap one of these tracks to start playing it.

Tap the bars at the top left to see other options for exploring music:

- ✔ Tap Radio to see a list of stations that other Spotify users have created.
- ✔ Tap Discover to see popular artists and albums.
- ✔ Tap Browse to go back to the genres list (refer to Figure 8-4).
- ✔ If you really like someone's Spotify selection, tap Follow to enjoy their complete playlist.

Figure 8-4: Listen to as much Spotify music as you like in Shuffle Play.

## How free and paid-for Spotify versions compare

You can get a paid version of Spotify that doesn't have adverts and that lets you select your own songs. This Spotify Premium subscription costs £9.99 per month. This version also lets you download songs and playlists to listen to even if your Hudl isn't online. You can listen to anything you download as long as you have an active Spotify Premium subscription. The service offers a 30-day trial so you can see whether it's for you. You'll see a green box at the bottom left of the Spotify screen suggesting you 'Get Premium for ad-free listening'. Tap this box to go to the upgrade page.

# Downloading Songs from a Music Subscription Service

You won't always be connected to the Internet when you want to listen to music on your Hudl, which is why the option to save stations in blinkbox music is handy. Another way to ensure you can always play your favourite songs is to buy songs through Google Play Music that are then saved on your Hudl. This way, you'll be able to listen to them whenever you want.

## Buying music from the Google Play Store

You can buy music whenever you like from the Google Play Store. Just follow these steps:

1. **Tap the Play Store icon at the bottom right of the Hudl screen and then tap Music.**

2. **Search for a specific artist, view a Genres list or browse Top Albums and Top Songs.**

   You can listen to a preview of anything before buying it.

3. **Tap the price of a song or album to buy it.**

4. **Check that your bank card number is correct (only the last four digits are shown) and then tap Buy to confirm the purchase (see Figure 8-5).**

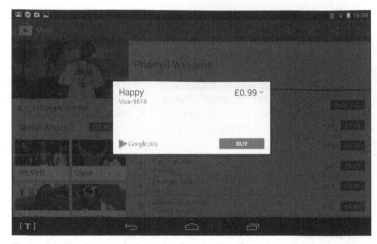

Figure 8-5: You buy music from the Google Play Store exactly the same way that you buy an app.

## Playing music bought from Google Play Music

To play music you've bought from Google Play Music, tap All Apps in the Favourites bar on your Home screen, and then tap the Play Music app icon.

If you want to, you can sign up for a free trial of Google's Listen Now service. Tap Got It to dismiss the message.

When your music library appears (see Figure 8-6), tap an album or song to play it, or tap I'm Feeling Lucky Mix if you'd like Google Play Music to create a playlist of music based on your recent listening history.

I'm feeling lucky mix

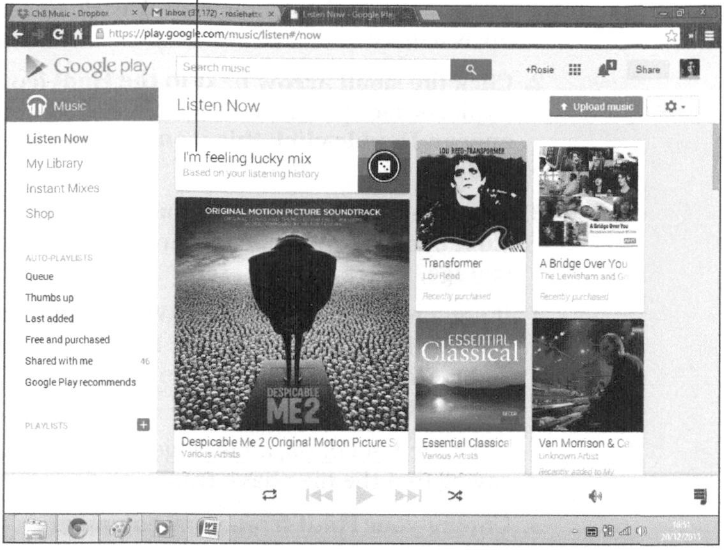

Figure 8-6: Tap a song or album to play it in the Play Music app.

# Moving Music That You Already Own to Your Hudl

You aren't limited to listening to music online or buying new albums. You can also listen to the music you already own on your Hudl.

## Transferring music from your computer

If you've got some music on your computer, you'll probably be keen to be able to listen to it on your Hudl too. You can do this very easily if you copy the music between the two devices via USB. Just follow these steps:

1. **Connect the two devices with the Hudl's micro-USB cable.**

   In a few seconds, the Hudl icon appears in the list of drives and devices on your PC on the left side of the

Explorer window. If you're using a Mac, you need to install Android File Transfer (www.android.com/filetransfer) on your Mac. The Hudl will show up as a drive.

2. **Click the small arrow next to the Hudl icon in the Explorer menu to make the internal storage icon appear. Double-click this icon and find the Music folder.**

3. **Drag the albums or tracks you want to copy to your Hudl over to the Music folder of the Hudl's internal storage.**

4. **If you prefer, you can open Windows Media Player on your PC and drag albums to the sync list on the right. Click the Sync tab to copy albums in the list to your Hudl.**

After a few seconds, a message appears on your Hudl, saying that the files have transferred.

5. **Unplug your Hudl from your computer.**

Wait until your music finishes copying over to your Hudl before unplugging the device from your computer. Some of the files may not arrive if you interrupt the process.

Tracks you upload from your computer appear in Google Play Music, along with any you buy through Play Music. In the next section, I explain how you can transfer iTunes songs and music bought from other MP3 services.

## Saving your music to your Google account

If you've got a sizable music collection stored on your computer, you probably don't want to spend ages copying it all to your Hudl. Luckily, a really simple option lets you access the music stored on your computer directly from your Hudl.

Google Play Music lets you store up to 20,000 songs in your Google account. Rather than transfer those songs from your computer to your Hudl, you can upload them to your Google account and then play them on your Hudl whenever you want to. Albums that you play frequently can be downloaded to your Hudl, where you can listen to them without needing web access.

To use Google Play Music, follow these steps:

1. **Download and install the Music Manager software for your computer from** `https://play.google.com/music/listen#/manager.`

2. **Sign in to your Google account.**

3. **Select the location on your computer where you store music.**

   You can upload music from iTunes, too. If you keep music in more than one place, choose Other and add the folders for each place manually.

4. **Choose Upload Songs to Google Play (see Figure 8-7).**

   Depending on how many albums you're uploading, the process could take an hour or two, particularly if Music Manager first re-encodes tracks so that they're saved as MP3 tracks, which Android devices such as the Hudl can play.

   Your songs are uploaded to your Google Play account and appear in the My Music folder in Google Play Music.

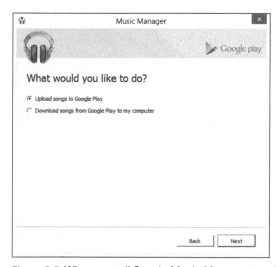

Figure 8-7: When you tell Google Music Manager to upload music from your computer it copies the music from your chosen folder to your Google account.

To listen to your music, just tap the Google Play app on the right side of the Hudl's Home screen. Then tap Music to open your music library (see Figure 8-8). Browse by artist, album or song, or search for a particular band or track, and tap any icon to play music.

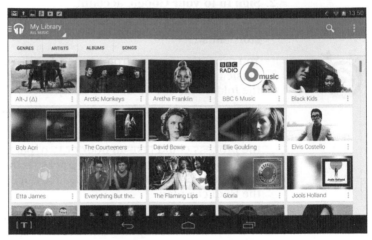

Figure 8-8: Google Play Music sorts your music collection by artist, album or song.

# 9

# Discovering Books and Magazines

*T*he Hudl is just the right size for reading. Its 7in screen is similar in size to a paperbook book, and its slim proportions make it ideal for slipping into a bag and sneaking in a few more pages of reading when you're able to. The long battery life also helps.

Google has made it very easy to buy books to download from its own Play Store, but the beauty of the Android system is that it's far from the only option. You can also buy books from your favourite online bookstores, and you may even be able to borrow books from your local library to read on your Hudl. You can also download books that are out of copyright for free from a website called Project Gutenberg (www.projectgutenberg.org).

You aren't limited to books, either. You can buy single copies or a subscription to a magazine or newspaper and flip the pages as though you were reading it on paper. If you prefer, you can download audiobooks and listen to a story instead.

# Buying and Reading Books on Your Hudl

The books you read on your Hudl are more than simply digitised versions of printed books. You can search them and add bookmarks to them, and they can remember the last page you read so you won't spend ages trying to remember where you got to. You can even look up words you don't recognise in an ebook (as digital books are referred to).

Before you can start reading ebooks and magazines on your Hudl, however, you need an app that can recognise the format they're created in and can display them on your tablet. The Hudl comes with two built-in apps that you can use to buy and read ebooks: blinkbox books and Google Play Books.

## Getting books from blinkbox books

blinkbox books is both a store to buy ebooks and an e-reader app, and is already installed on your Hudl. You can access blinkbox books from All Apps on the Favourites bar or from the blinkbox widget. Alternatively, tap the [T] at the bottom left of the Hudl's screen, swipe through the screens until you get to blinkbox books, and then tap Read.

The first time you use blinkbox books, you need to tap Register on the first screen (where you see the option to Sign In or Register).Type your name, email address and choose a password to create a blinkbox books account. If you have a Tesco Clubcard enter your Clubcard number to earn points on your book purchases. You must be connected to Wi-Fi to create and sign in to your account.

If you've already set up a blinkbox books account, just type in the email address and password you used for it.

After you log in you see your blinkbox books library, where you'll find books you've purchased or downloaded. Books in your library are organised by books you're reading, books you've yet to start reading and books you've finished reading.

To browse, sample or buy books from blinkbox, tap the Shop icon in the top right corner of the blinkbox books app. The blinkbox bookstore is organised by Fiction Top 100, Non-Fiction Top 100 and Categories (see Figure 9-1). You can search the bookstore by author, title or topic.

Figure 9-1: blinkbox books are organised by fiction, non-fiction and book category.

When you find a title you're interested in, tap the book cover to go to the information page for that book (see Figure 9-2). The page shows a synopsis of the book, information about the author and a sample extract from the beginning of the book.

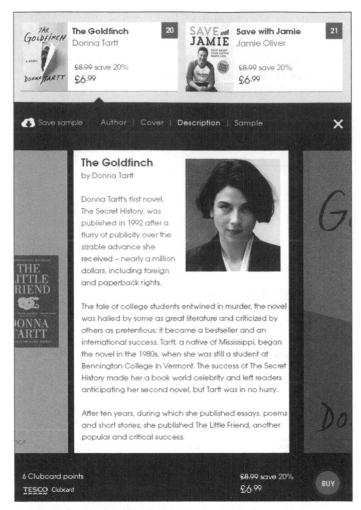

Figure 9-2: Tap the book's cover to see the synopsis page.

After you've selected a book to purchase, tap Buy in the bottom right corner of the book description screen.

If you are a new customer a pop-up screen appears asking you to provide your card details so that you can buy the book. Tap Add New Card and type in your payment details and then tap Pay Now. You will receive a confirmation email of your purchase.

# Reading books in the blinkbox books app

Books you buy from blinkbox books appear in your library. The library appears when you open the blinkbox books app (see Figure 9-3), and you can access it from within the app by tapping the blinkbox logo in the top left corner of the app. Books you've bought but have not yet downloaded to your Hudl have a cloud icon on them to show that they are saved to your account but are stored 'in the cloud' and aren't currently on your Hudl. Tap Options⇨Download when you want to download and read each book.

To open a book, tap its thumbnail. The book will open and show the front cover in full-screen mode. Tap the right side of the book's cover to go to the first page or the contents page. To move back by a page, tap the left side of the page displayed.

**Figure 9-3:** Tap Library when logged in to blinkbox books to see your books.

The blinkbox books app automatically bookmarks the page you're on when you stop reading. The next time you open the book, it will automatically open to the last page you read.

To jump to a later point in the book, tap anywhere on the screen in blinkbox books and tap the options icon that appears in the top right hand corner of the screen. Then tap the table of contents that appears in the top right corner of the screen; you can go to the start of any chapter by tapping the chapter number or name.

You'll probably find it most natural to turn the Hudl to portrait mode when you're reading, just like you would read a paper book.

The high resolution of the Hudl's screen and good backlight mean that the pages of your book should be easy to read. You can make books easier to read in the blinkbox books app by changing the text size, font, page colour and page layout. To access the display settings, tap anywhere on the page to display the Options icon at the top right. Tap the 'Aa' icon to bring up the list of display settings (see Figure 9-4).

Use the + and – arrows to change the text size and the slider to adjust the screen's brightness. Tap the small arrow next to Font Options to open the list of font choices. Tap a font option to select it. You can also change the page margins and line spacing and choose a different background colour for the page by tapping the respective options.

You might want to wait to download a book until you're ready to read it if you've also downloaded lots of apps and films to your Hudl and it's getting short of storage space. If this is the case, consider deleting items you no longer need to store on your Hudl.

To delete a book from your Hudl, go into the Library, tap Options beneath the book cover and then tap Remove Book from Device. You can download a book again by going to the blinkbox books Library and tapping Options beneath the book you want to download.

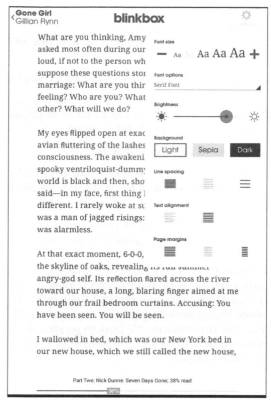

**Figure 9-4:** You can change the font, text size, line spacing and page brightness in the blinkbox books app to make pages easier to read.

# Buying books from the Google Play Store

Google also has an e-reader tool, the Play Books app, already installed on your Hudl. You can buy books from the Google Play Store to read on the Play Books app by following these steps:

1. **Tap the Google Play icon in the bottom right of the Hudl's Home screen.**

2. **Tap Books in the categories section of the store.**

3. **Browse the book offerings.**

The store has thousands of books to choose from, including out-of-copyright classics that you can download for free and an indifferent selection of free books by new authors.

4. **Tap Free Sample to download an excerpt of a book.**

   Many books by established authors offer a free sample or chapter as a taster. The number of pages you get to preview varies from book to book.

5. **Tap a book's price to buy it.**

6. **Tap Buy to confirm the last four digits of your bank card are correct and to proceed with the book purchase.**

   The book downloads to your Hudl and appears in the My Books section of your Google Play account.

It's best not to let children loose in the Google Play Store, as a lot of erotic fiction is on offer (especially in the Bestsellers section), and some of the covers and titles leave little to the imagination! Unfortunately, you can't apply specific filters or settings. For this reason, it's best to go straight to the children's section, where you can help your child choose a suitable book to read.

## Using the Play Books e-reader app

When you download a book from the Google Play Books store and tap Open, the book opens in the Play Books app. (You can also access this app by tapping All Apps in the Favourites bar.) The cover page is displayed full-screen; tap the screen to go to the first page of the book or to the contents page. To move on to the next page, tap in the bottom right corner of the screen. The page number is shown at the bottom of the screen when you tap the Hudl's screen.

To jump forward a few pages, drag the slider to the right. To go the contents page, title page or introduction, tap the menu icon at the bottom left of the Play Books app screen and tap the option you want. The same menu also has an option to go to any bookmarks you've created within your book. You can bookmark a page you're on by tapping the options at the top right of the screen and tapping Add Bookmark.

You can also add notes and highlights to pages and portions of text. Tap the page icon with the plus sign next to it to create a note. When the note appears, type whatever you want to append to the page. To highlight a passage, tap and hold your finger on the screen and then tap the yellow highlighter dot.

You can also search within books in Play Books. To do so, tap anywhere onscreen and then tap the magnifying glass that appears. Type your search term in the search box that displays at the top of the screen and then tap the magnifying glass on the Hudl's keyboard to start the search.

To adjust the size of the text while you're reading, tap the screen and then tap 'Aa' at the top right to bring up a menu of useful options (see Figure 9-5). You can change the font size, space between lines, typeface and screen brightness. A Sans (for *sans-serif*) font is usually easier to read than a serif font because the characters don't have swirly flourishes. Tap the book area of the screen to make the menu disappear. Unless you change the settings again, any books you open from now on use the same text size, font and line spacing.

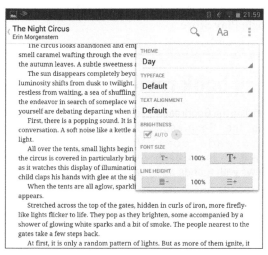

Figure 9-5: You can change the default font, text size and brightness in the Play Books app.

# Downloading Other ebook Software

The best-known e-reader app is Kindle (the name refers to both the app and a standalone e-reader device). The Kindle app is free and can be used on your Hudl as well as on other devices. You can download the Kindle app from the Google Play Store. You'll need a Kindle account to log in. If you already have an account, any books already in your Kindle account will be shown once you've logged in.

Another good e-reader option is Aldiko. You can use Aldiko to open and read books you download from Project Gutenberg or buy through an online bookstore.

If you like reading comics and graphic novels, you'll need an app that can open books in the comic file format. I recommend the free Comics app which has a library of more than 40,000 comics that you can buy individually or read as part of a subscription.

You can download the Aldiko and Comics apps for free from the Google Play Store.

## Consulting book reviews before buying

I recommend installing the Goodreads app or visiting the Goodreads site (www.goodreads.com), as you can use it to share book ratings and reviews with friends and other site users. You also may want to investigate Lovereading UK (www.lovereading.co.uk), which offers author previews as well as book reviews and tip-offs.

# Reading Magazines and Newspapers

Your Hudl offers lots of options for catching up on the latest news and magazines.

## Browsing the Newsstand

You can buy magazines and newspapers from the Google Play Store just as easily as you can buy books and music. The only difference is that when you open the Google Play app, you tap Newsstand rather than Books.

The Newsstand often has free issues of magazines on offer. To find a magazine, either search for it by title or browse the Categories or Top Magazines section. Tap a magazine's cover to find out more about it (see Figure 9-6). Above the price are details about any trial offer. Tap the Buy Issue button to buy a single issue, or tap Subscribe to buy an ongoing subscription.

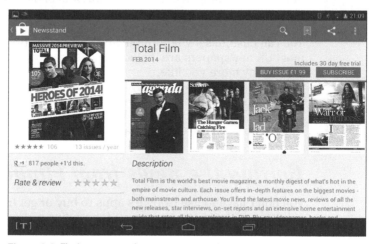

**Figure 9-6:** Find out more about a magazine by tapping its Newsstand cover.

Make sure that you check the details of any trial offer you take up. Sometimes you'll be offered a free issue, but as soon as the trial period expires, the subscription kicks in automatically, and you end up paying per issue with no further notice. Also check how long the minimum subscription period is.

After you buy a magazine, you'll find it in the My Newsstand section of Google Play. If you purchase a subscription, new issues are added automatically.

You can buy newspapers through the Newsstand, too, or you can go straight to the newspaper listings by tapping My News. Tap Explore in this section to see lots more publications organised by interest area, from politics to parenting and science. When you tap on one of these categories you see a selection of news sources and magazines to choose from.

To view the latest news stories, tap the Read Now section of the Newsstand. Read Now is a combination of the Google Play magazine store and Google Currents, which displays news items that other Google users are sharing.

An advantage of using Read Now is that the stories are laid out to suit reading on a tablet, without lots of distracting elements spread all over the screen.

You can customise which publications' stories appear but most UK newspapers are included, so it's really a matter of adding any more you like.

Many newspapers have websites where you can read their stories for free, and their apps usually are free too. Download those apps from the Google Play Store.

## Getting the news from Flipboard

You don't have to use Google's apps to buy or get free periodicals. One of the best-known apps for reading news stories is Flipboard (`https://flipboard.com`), which has a free app you can download from the Google Play Store. When you sign up for a free Flipboard account (or log in using your Facebook details), you can customise the news feeds you see. You can combine updates from friends you follow on Facebook and Twitter, too, as well as save items to read later and share with friends.

Rather than tap your way around the pages in Flipboard, you swipe to flip them, like flicking through a newspaper or magazine.

To customise your Flipboard, swipe across the main Flipboard splash screen; then, on the next screen, tick any categories that interest you (see Figure 9-7). When you've ticked everything you want to see, tap Build Your Flipboard.

Figure 9-7: Choose which topics interest you, and Flipboard shows you relevant articles.

The next several screens explain that you can further refine your choices and add Facebook updates by creating a free account. If you prefer, however, you can just move on to seeing what Flipboard does. Tap a category on the Cover Stories screen and then flip through the headlines until you come to something of interest.

## Browsing magazines in Zinio

If you want magazines rather than news stories, I recommend trying Zinio (www.zinio.com). Many magazines that aren't in the Google Play Newsstand are available through Zinio (mainly because it's been around much longer), which offers more than 5,000 titles.

To use Zinio, download and open the free Zinio app; then tap a category on the left side of the screen. When the subcategories appear, tap a magazine's title to find out more about it. Then you can buy a single issue or start a subscription (see Figure 9-8). When you tap Buy This Issue or Subscribe, you'll be prompted to join Zinio or sign in to your Zinio account.

Zinio also has lots of free articles you can read without needing to create a Zinio account. To find these articles, tap the eye icon at the top right of the main page.

As with other apps, you can zoom a page in Zinio by double-tapping it or by pinching and pushing your fingers away from each other. You can't customise the text size and typeface, however.

**Figure 9-8:** Zinio sells many magazines you won't find in the Google Play Newsstand.

# Listening to Audiobooks on Your Hudl

In addition to reading books on your Hudl, you can have books read to you. The audiobooks site Audible (www.audible.co.uk) works on a subscription basis, and you can download an Audible for Android app from the Google Play Store.

 Audible is owned by Amazon.com, so if you've already got an Amazon account, you just need to sign in to it to start using Audible.

To listen to an audiobook in the Audible app, tap Device at the top of the screen. You may find that the Hudl's speaker is loud enough that you can listen to the narration without needing to use headphones, but you may want to speed or slow down the narration. To do this, tap the speedometer icon at the top of the screen; then tap 0.5 to make it slower or a multiplier to speed it up (see Figure 9-9).

Figure 9-9: Fancy a bedtime story? Listening to audiobooks is a great way of using your Hudl.

If you decide that you like listening to audiobooks, you can start an Audible subscription, which costs £3.99 a month for the first three months and then £7.99 a month for one audiobook or £14.99 for two audiobooks a month.

# 10

# Games and Entertainment

*In This Chapter*

▶ Playing games with the whole family

▶ Bringing children's TV characters to life

▶ Getting creative on the Hudl

*Y*our Hudl can entertain you in all manner of ways. You can waste hours watching online videos of course, but you have plenty of games and quizzes to enjoy too. You don't need a Wi-Fi connection to play most of them, either, because you can simply download these apps to your Hudl.

The Google Play Store stocks thousands of games, many of them free. In this chapter, I suggest a few that you and your family may enjoy, from classic board, racing and card games to action and role-playing games. Some of these action games are rather gory, which is why the games industry gives them age ratings. Download the Game Ratings by ESRB (Entertainment Software Rating Board) app from the Google Play Store to see the age rating for any game. To use it, you just type the game's name into the app's search box. You might find this app useful if your child mentions a game they want to play, but you have concerns about its suitability.

Another easy way to check whether a game is going to be too graphic for your child is to check its content rating on Google Play. When you visit the description page for the game, you'll see information about how many times it's been downloaded and when it was last updated. Next to this is the Content Rating. FIFA

14 is rated as suitable for everyone, but Grand Theft Auto: San Andreas is shown as High Maturity, which means it may contain graphic violence, swearing and adult content.

I recommend you turn on Content Filtering in Settings (which I describe in Chapter 3), because it makes games designed for older audiences incompatible with your Hudl. This means that even if your child searches for a High Maturity game by name, if you've applied a content filter, the Hudl won't be able to find it.

All the games and other apps in this chapter are available from the Google Play Store, which you can access by tapping the Play icon at the bottom right of the Hudl's Home screen. In the Play Store, tap Games and type in the title or type of the game you want to find, or browse the Top New or Top Free games categories to find one to play. Unless otherwise stated, each game mentioned is free.

# Games for (Mostly) All Ages

Games are much more fun when you've got someone to play against. This chapter describes some great games you can play on your Hudl against friends or online opponents.

## Classic board games

Your Hudl gives you a new way to play some classic board games such as Ludo, Scrabble, Trivial Pursuit and Pictionary as well as lots of card games. There's even a version of the popular TV game show *Countdown*.

Many board games let you pass-and-play. This option is ideal for playing at home as you can take your turn and then pass the Hudl to the next person.

### Scrabble

Scrabble is free to download and offers several game-play options. When you first open Scrabble, you get the option to play online with friends and share your scores on Facebook, but I found it easiest to start in single-player mode and compete against the built-in opponent.

To place a tile on the Scrabble board, tap and drag it to the square where you want it to go. When the word has been constructed, tap Play to confirm your choice.

 If you're not sure of a spelling, you can look up the word by tapping Dictionary. The 'teacher' you play against often tells you that you could have scored much more highly and then suggests a word that doesn't appear in the English lexicon as we know it.

## Sporcle

If you want to play web-based games, try Sporcle (www. sporcle.com). The site offers thousands of quick quizzes (see Figure 10-1) and even lets you create your own quizzes for other people to try. (You can also download the Sporcle app.)

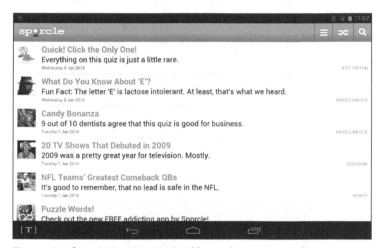

Figure 10-1: Sporcle has thousands of free quizzes you can play on your Hudl.

## Facebook games

One of the best ways to play against friends is to do so through Facebook (www.facebook.com; see Chapter 5). Log in to Facebook and tap the Games and Apps link on the left side of your profile page to see a list of the most popular games that friends are playing through Facebook. You can also see which of your friends have installed a particular game, which makes it easy to find online opponents.

To choose a game, tap it and install it on your Hudl (via the Google Play Store).

Popular Facebook games include Words With Friends (see Figure 10-2), Candy Crush Saga and Pet Rescue Saga.

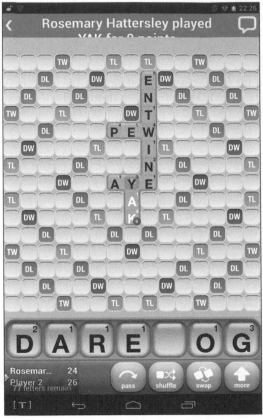

Figure 10-2: You can play games such as Words With Friends via Facebook.

## Fast-paced puzzle games

Playing against the clock can make puzzles more compelling. You'll find plenty of Tetris-like games to download and play on your Hudl.

Some games are brain-training games of a sort, because they test your mental reflexes as you play, so it's worth searching 'mind games' or 'brain training' for fun games too.

### Candy Crush Saga

Candy Crush Saga is one of the most popular games of the moment. You can play it online or download the app. You have to move jelly beans and other sweets around to form lines that then get crushed and disappear. It's simple to play but hard to put down. Be warned!

### Cut the Rope

In this challenging game, you must keep Om Nom, the little green monster, fed with candy by cutting the rope holding it in the right place and simultaneously getting the candy wheel to pick up as many stars as it can on its descent. Working out where to chop and where the candy will fall seems simple at first, but Cut the Rope has hundreds of increasingly complex levels to work through.

## Racing games

The Hudl's gyroscope comes into its own when you're racing around a track.

### Real Racing 3

In Real Racing 3 (see Figure 10-3), you just grip the sides of your tablet and steer smoothly — but ever so quickly — through the bends of Suzuka, Nürburgring and other well-known tracks. The game features a choice of cars you can customise, recognisable tracks from around the world and the opportunity to race other people for a chance on the leaderboard.

### Angry Birds Go

Angry Birds Go is a racing game built on the chaotic cartoon characters from the extremely popular game series Angry Birds. Your character is catapulted down the track, careening into gold coins and bashing into other players as he goes. It's ridiculously fun.

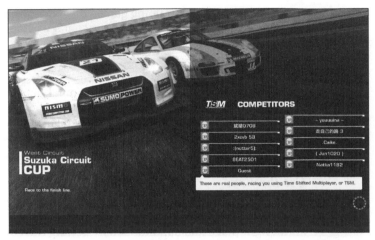

Figure 10-3: In Real Racing 3 you can race against real opponents.

### Trial Xtreme 3

Take your motorbike off road and put your stunt-riding skills to the test as you leap from obstacle to obstacle on assault courses and over dirt tracks. Trial Xtreme 3 is one of the most exhilarating games you can play.

## Sports games

If you're a sports fan, you'll find plenty of trivia quizzes on the Google Play Store and at Sporcle.com to test your knowledge. You can even manage your own team with the excellent SEGA Football Manager or EA's free FIFA 14.

### FIFA 14

FIFA 14 is more than just a football manager — you can manouevre your players around the pitch and help line up shots on goal as well as getting involved in bidding wars with other managers for the best players. You'll quickly know whether you've made the right choice as the live commentary lets you know how well you're doing. You've a choice of more than 600 teams and 16,000 players and can follow their real-world fixtures too.

# Adventure and role-playing games

You can build and explore new worlds on your Hudl or become a hero saving the worlds you find yourself thrust into.

## Clash of Clans

Clash of Clans is a role-playing strategy game in which you must build a stronghold (see Figure 10-4), train your troops and then do battle with neighbouring clans to protect your gold and other resources, and to pillage their riches. Once you've mastered the basics, you can pit your strategic wits against other clans across the world using the Hudl's Wi-Fi connection.

Figure 10-4: In Clash of Clans you build a stronghold and then take your battle to neighbouring clans.

## Minecraft – Pocket Edition

If you like to build your own worlds, Minecraft – Pocket Edition is likely to pique your interest. From basic building blocks similar to Lego blocks, you can create whole worlds. Then you can post videos of your painstakingly designed worlds and characters to share with friends.

## Restricting in-app purchases

You may have heard that some games ask you to pay for items as you play. These items are known as *in-app purchases*. Fortunately, you must type your password to confirm in-app purchases, and your Hudl has password protection for app purchases already set up, so you needn't worry about accidental purchases. You can check that this feature is still switched on by tapping the top-right menu in Google Play and choosing Settings. If the Password option is ticked under User Controls (see the following figure), you'll be prompted for a password whenever you try to buy a paid-for app or buy an item within an app or game. This setting can be controlled separately for each account on the Hudl.

When you've typed your password to confirm that you want to buy something in an app, you'll be able to make purchases for the next 30 minutes without having to provide your password again. Bear this timeframe in mind if you've just downloaded a game for your child to play and he or she starts playing it immediately. Most games aimed at very young children have a prompt to get an adult to confirm purchases, but not all do.

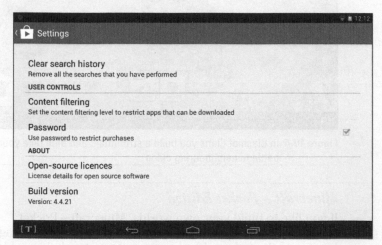

# Children's Games

From colour-matching and shape-recognition to counting and songs, there are lots of fun educational games for kids in the Google Play Store.

# TV-based games

You can find many apps and games that are based on children's TV programmes. In particular, *Peppa Pig* and *The Gruffalo* have spawned lots of games based on their characters.

Nearly 40 games are devoted to Peppa Pig, including number and shape-recognition games, jigsaws and mini action games. One of my family's favourites is Peppa Pig's Holiday. This £2.99 app takes you to the seaside, where you have to design ice creams, create postcards (see Figure 10-5) and count the suitcases to make sure you have them all. Peppa Pig's Holiday also has songs and a sticker album you add to by playing the mini games.

**Figure 10-5:** In Peppa Pig's Holiday you design postcards to send home.

# Interactive games

Interactive books, which are halfway between books and games, are listed in the Apps section of the Google Play Store. Some of these books simply narrate the story; others have fun interactive elements.

In Chuggington Chug Patrol, for example, you must clear the railway tracks of fallen trees and logs and help pull another train out of trouble (see Figure 10-6). You need to pay to unlock additional adventures.

Figure 10-6: Chuggington Chug Patrol is a CBeebies TV favourite that comes to life in an interactive storybook.

You'll find a good selection of interactive storybooks by searching for 'storybooks' at the Google Play Store.

## Silly fun

It can be fun to use the Hudl's microphone to find information, but it can be even more fun to speak into the microphone and hear what you've just said repeated back to you in a funny parrot's or cat's voice!

Talking Tomcat is one of the most popular entertainment apps for Android. Just tap the screen to get the animated cat to listen, and tap again when you've finished. The cat immediately repeats what you just said in his own style.

Once you tire of Talking Tomcat, you can try other talking animals such as Talking Pierre the Parrot. The app has a child mode that ensures Pierre doesn't repeat any rude words. You need to pay to unlock some of the items in this app.

## Creativity Apps

Many apps make it easy to get creative with your Hudl, from writing stories to making videos and slideshows to programming your own music.

# Drawing and painting

Children thoroughly enjoy the drawing and creative apps you can download for your Hudl. Here are some drawing apps you could use with yours.

For greater accuracy, it's really worth investing in a digital pen or stylus. These devices cost as little as £5 each and they greatly enhance the sketching and colouring-in experience.

### Drawing Pad

Drawing Pad is one of the best drawing apps for younger users. The app provides a blank canvas to draw on and a selection of fine-tipped pencils, crayons and marker pens to use. An eraser lets users undo lines that go astray or add quirky effects. Children will also enjoy the fun selection of stickers that they can drag into place and resize to create a collage. If they like, they can combine stickers and their own drawn designs.

### Crayola DigiTools Paint

Crayola's DigiTools painting app makes drawings come to life when finished. Birds take flight, and catwalk creations strut their stuff. Paid-for upgrades add more painting tools, stencils and stamps.

### Comic Strip It! Lite

It's always fun to put yourself in a story, and with comic strip apps and games, you can do so easily. Comic Strip It! Lite provides several comic strip layouts in which you can customise the characters, edit the speech bubbles and add photos from your Hudl Gallery.

# Sketching and photo effects

One of the most rewarding ways to use your Hudl is to open a sketching app and use it as a freeform sketchpad. It's also great fun getting artistic with your favourite photos.

### Sketch Guru

Sketch Guru is a brilliant free app that adds sketching and watercolour effects to your photos. All you need to do is open a photo from your Gallery or Google Drive or take a new photo with the Hudl's camera. Then you can use Sketch Guru to apply a range of painting effects (see Figure 10-7). Use the settings slider to adjust how marked the transformation is.

Figure 10-7: Give your photos a makeover with Sketch Guru.

## SketchBook Express

SketchBook Express is a professional drawing tool from Autodesk, with plenty of very fine brushes on offer. Using these brushes, you can draw very delicately even if you don't have a digital stylus.

# *Music-making*

The Hudl makes a great digital instrument. You can use it as a piano keyboard, as a synthesiser or as a drum pad. You'll find a good choice of instrument apps in the Google Play Store, some of which include tuition modules and sample sheet music or guitar tabs. For more free music to practice playing, you need only look online.

If you've got a 'real' instrument, your Hudl can show you how to play it. Apps such as Guitar Lessons Free provide app-based tuition, and lots of free tutorials are available at YouTube (www.youtube.com) and the great video how-to site Videojug (www.videojug.com).

## *Perfect Piano*

Perfect Piano is a really good music app to get started with. It has a choice of pianos, drums and guitars and lets you play multiple keyboards at the same time (see Figure 10-8). It also includes free sheet music that you can save to the app and then play along with. You can change the playback speed so you can keep up.

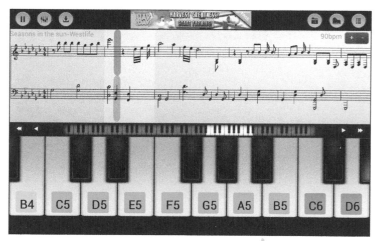

**Figure 10-8:** Make music your way with Perfect Piano.

### Karaoke

Karaoke is another popular way to express your musical talents on your Hudl. If you search for 'karaoke' in the Google Play Store, you'll find lots of free apps containing backing music and lyric sheets for songs from many countries.

For the One Direction or Justin Bieber fan in your family, themed karaoke apps are available to download.

Most karaoke apps let you record and even export what you sing, so you could remix your vocals in one of the free music-mixing apps for your Hudl and add them to a track you play using a free instrument app.

# 11

# Using Your Hudl to Get Organised

*C*hapter 2 discusses how to set up a Google account so you can send and receive emails and manage all aspects of your Hudl. This chapter is where you discover just how useful Google's extensive services are and how well they work together.

As you use your Hudl you may come across a screen asking whether you want to install Google Now, a tool that brings together several of the other Google services you may use. (You can also access Google Now by holding your finger on the Home button and swiping up to the word Google that appears above it.) If you allow Google to take note of your location, for example, Google Now can provide weather, travel, restaurant and entertainment information that's local to you.

Your Hudl includes lots of other useful tools to help you organise your diary, remember appointments and plan how to get to places. Google Maps not only shows you how to get there, but also tells you the precise details of your journey and what the destination looks like.

# Setting an Alarm on Your Hudl

As I explain in Chapter 13, you can customise your Hudl by adding a digital or analogue clock to one of its screens. To do this, go into All Apps from the Favourites bar and tap Widgets and select either Analogue Clock or Digital Clock. Hold your finger on your chosen widget and drag it to a space on one of the Hudl's Home screens. Now tap the clock widget to open it, and then tap the alarm clock icon at the bottom left to call up Alarms. Tap the + at the top right to add a new alarm, and type in the time you want the alarm to go off. Finally, tap OK to set the alarm.

# Using the Calendar App

The Calendar app comes with your Hudl and is found in All Apps. It's the pale blue-and-white icon with '31' written on it. If you want to, drag this icon to one of the Hudl's Home screens so you can access it more easily.

Tap to open the Calendar app. It shows today's date at the top right and the month at the top left, with the current week on view (see Figure 11-1). You can always get back to today's listings by tapping Today at the top right. Swipe right to left across the screen to see what's happening next week.

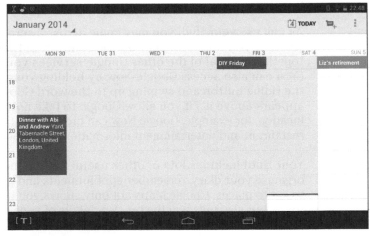

**Figure 11-1:** The Calendar colour-codes your week's events.

Calendar usually shows weeks starting on a Monday, but you can change this setting by tapping the menu at the top right and then tapping Settings⇨General Settings⇨Week Starts On. Change Locale Default to another day.

# Creating a Family Calendar

You can easily share your Calendar with other people by sending them an email from your calendar requesting access to their email calendars. This action joins your calendars. If you prefer, though, you can also use a dedicated app to share your plans — handy if you aren't all using Google email accounts.

Cozi Family Calendar is a family planner that everyone can contribute to. One advantage is that it's non-hierarchical, so anyone can add items or amend them. Events and appointments are colour-coded (as you see in Figure 11-2) so you can see what everyone's doing or simply browse through your own appointments and to-do lists.

To set up your shared calendar, just use your own email address as the basis, or create a new email account just for sharing. The advantage of setting up a dedicated email address for the Cozi family planner is that you only get notifications about your own appointments and tasks, rather than seeing the updates everyone makes. Each person logs in to the Cozi calendar to add or amend events.

## Creating an event

To create an event, follow these steps:

1. **Tap Calendar.**

2. **Tap the + at the top right.**

3. **Type the appointment name and then tap the time it takes place.**

4. **Tap the date and time to change the day and duration, if you want.**

5. **Tap Done to add the event to the calendar.**

If you want to be reminded of an appointment, tap Edit⇨ Reminder, choose how long in advance you want to be emailed about the appointment and then tap Done.

Figure 11-2: Cozi Family Planner makes it easy to keep track of everyone's diary.

Unless you untick the All option when you create a new event, Cozi adds the event to everyone's calendars. When you've added more people to your shared calendar, you can select their names from the list of people to whom an appointment applies. Each person gets an email about their events and is assigned a colour denoting them on the Cozi calendar.

## Adding calendar widgets to a Home screen

Handily, Cozi comes with calendar and to-do list widgets that you can place on the Hudl's Home screen. To use them, tap All Apps on the Favourites bar, tap the Widgets tab, find the Cozi widget you want to use and drag it to a free space on one of the Hudl's Home screens (see Figure 11-3). Now you can jump straight from that Home screen to the full calendar or to-do list.

Figure 11-3: Add a calendar widget to a Home screen for an at-a-glance diary check.

## Organising your shopping with Cozi

Cozi has a Shopping section where family members can add their own entries, which should prevent complaints about anyone's favourite brand of cereal or shower gel being forgotten the next time you shop at Tesco. You can add these extras to your regular grocery order.

As you see in Chapter 12, the Tesco Groceries app remembers the products you order regularly and what you chose last time, so shopping no longer needs to be a chore.

# Saving Web Pages and Keeping Notes on Your Hudl

When you come across an item of interest online or a website you visit often, you can save the page or site so you can to go back to it later. To do this, just tap the star at the right end of the web address bar. You may want to bookmark the BBC News website or one of its sections, for example (see Figure 11-4). You can rename the label for the web page in the Add Bookmark box, if you want to; otherwise, just tap Save. To see your bookmarks, tap the menu at the top right and then tap Bookmarks.

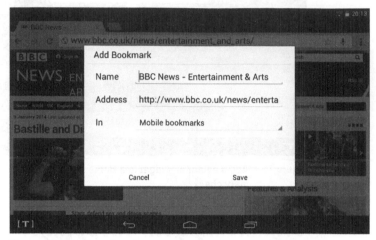

Figure 11-4: Bookmark web pages you want to return to frequently.

## Finding items online faster

Tabs are also really useful tools. If you tap the grey tab next to the name of the website you're currently browsing (or tap New Tab in the top-right Chrome menu), a new tab appears, and the web page you were on before is simply pushed behind it. On the new tab, simply type the address of another website you want to visit or tap Most Visited, Bookmarks or Other Devices.

Most Visited shows you the websites you go to most frequently, which makes it easy to get to them again. Other Devices shows you any other laptops, tablets or phones you use to browse the web while logged in to your Google account and when it was last synchronised. This option only works with the Google Chrome browser, but it's handy because if you use any Google services on other gadgets, you'll be able to see your search results and details of any places you've looked up in Google Maps without having to start a new search for them.

## Saving web pages offline

Chrome is really good at remembering what you did last time you were online and showing you the same web pages and searches without needing to be prompted. Often, however, you'll want to save items and use them when your Hudl isn't connected to the Internet. For this purpose, I recommend the Evernote app (`www.evernote.com`).

Evernote is a fantastic app for all sorts of note-taking and organisational tasks. It even offers a calendar and to-do list. Evernote is particularly useful if you often save web pages or take notes, because these items are collated and stored within a binder. If you type a note in Evernote on your Hudl, that note is automatically added to your Evernote binder. After an item has been saved to your Evernote account, you can view and search everything within it, so if you've saved a recipe or reviews of a hotel you want to book, you can call them up whenever you want to.

To use Evernote, just download and open the app; then follow the onscreen instructions to create and set up your account. After this you'll be able to use the Jot function to take notes. You don't even need to save your notes as you go, so if you get a chance to type only a snippet before you're interrupted, Evernote still has a copy of it. If you don't assign a name to a note, Evernote labels it with your location, time and date of its creation. You can change this setting at any time by tapping the name field and overwriting it. You can even record a voice memo. To do this, just tap the microphone on the main Evernote screen (see Figure 11-5).

Because it's so useful for taking notes and storing important documents, you may find yourself saving financial and other personal information in Evernote. Evernote is very secure, but you should add a PIN code to it if you're going to use it as a document safe. To do so, you need to upgrade to the Premium version of Evernote, which costs $4 a month or $35 a year.

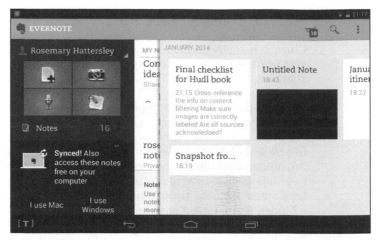

Figure 11-5: Evernote is brilliant for writing notes and recording voice memos.

## Scanning and saving documents in Evernote

You can also use your Hudl as a scanner and save documents as notes (see Figure 11-6). This feature can be useful for keeping copies of shopping receipts, bills and other important items. To take a snapshot of a paper document, tap the camera icon on the left of the Evernote screen; then hold your Hudl over the page you want to photograph.

 You can also initiate this option by tapping the paper-clip icon at the top right of a note and choosing Paper Camera from the resulting menu.

If you need to, use the slider at the bottom to zoom in. Tap the green button to take the shot. The page is saved and clipped to the newest note you created.

You can take a series of photos this way, and Evernote attaches them all to the same note. Then you can scroll through all of them seamlessly.

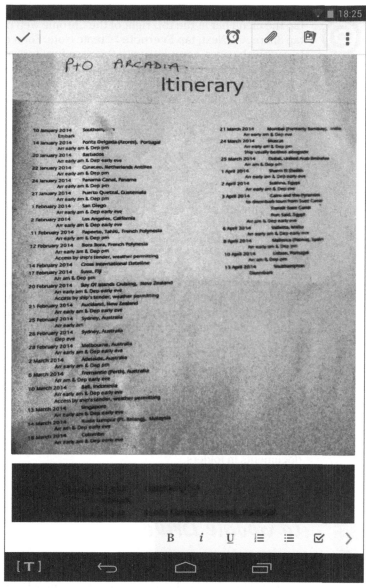

Figure 11-6: Evernote can save snapshots of your printed documents.

To save web pages in Evernote, browse to that site as usual then tap the menu bar at the top right of the Chrome web page and tap Share . . . . Next, tap Evernote⇨Create Note. For a quicker way to save web pages, complete with the page furniture and formatting, install the free EverClip app and sign in to your Evernote account from it. Thereafter, you can simply tap Save at the top right of a web page to save the whole page to your Evernote binder.

# Saving Items to Your Hudl

As I mention in several chapters, it's really easy to save items you've bought or received by email. Photos and videos taken on your Hudl are also saved on it. In most cases, you can simply tap and hold an item and then tap Save to save it to your Hudl.

You may worry, however, about what happens to all these items if you lose your Hudl for some reason. In Chapter 13, I suggest installing Lookout (www.lookout.com) as a precaution because it can help relocate your missing tablet and, if needs be, wipe its contents remotely.

For everyday convenience, you can simply use the free Google Drive to back up the contents of your Hudl. This way, you can download anything you need to and can easily manage the storage space on your Hudl. Drive stores 15GB worth of photos, videos, music and documents for free, and you can pay for additional space. It's really useful for organising your photos and documents in folders.

## Saving your Hudl's contents to Google Drive

Drive is already loaded on your Hudl, so you just need to go to All Apps on the Favourites bar and tap the Drive icon to open it. Then follow these steps to start a new Drive:

1. **Tap Next.**

2. **Tap Create on the bottom menu.**

The next screen gives you the option to create folders, documents or spreadsheets to be saved to your Google account automatically.

3. **Tap Folder, type a folder name and then tap OK.**

4. **Tap Upload, and choose what you want to add to your Google Drive (see Figure 11-7).**

Figure 11-7: Once uploaded from your Hudl, your photos appear in your Google Drive folder.

You probably won't want to save everything that's on your Hudl. In most cases, the contents are saved within the app and are simply downloaded again with the app if you reinstall it. For items that you definitely want to save and that are only on your Hudl, it's worth making sure that you tap the Share icon (the connected white dots in the top right of the screen) and then tap the Drive icon.

If you find yourself using Drive often, you may want to drag the Drive icon onto a Home screen for easy access.

You can make items that you add to your Drive available offline by tapping the information icon at the top right (the 'i' in a circle) and then tapping Available Offline to set it to On. You can also share items in your Drive with friends by adding their email address in the Who Has Access section (see Figure 11-8).

Figure 11-8: To share an item individually from your Google Drive, tap the item and then add your friends' email addresses.

## Sharing and creating documents in Drive

Although Drive is a useful place to store items, it's also a document creation and collaboration tool. To create a document, tap Create⇨Document at the bottom of the Drive screen, name your document and start typing. To edit the document, tap anywhere within it; the Hudl's keyboard appears so you can start typing (see Figure 11-9). Tap Done when you finish making changes.

To share your document, tap the information icon at top right and then add the email address of anyone who you'd like to be able to view and edit it. If you just want that person to be able to view the document, not to make any changes to it, tap his or her name in the sharing list, change the setting from Can Edit to Can View and then tap OK.

If someone shares items with you through Google Drive, you'll be able to see this fact by tapping your user account name at the top left of the Drive screen and then tapping Shared With Me.

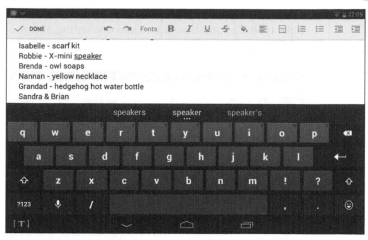

Figure 11-9: You can create, edit and share documents in Drive.

# Planning Your Travels with Your Hudl

Google Maps is an incredibly useful tool for finding out where places are, checking the distances between locations and finding out the best way to get from A to B. What's particularly impressive is that you can see photos of your destination.

To get travel information, first make sure that Location Services is active on your Hudl. You can easily tell whether it is because as soon as you open Google Maps, it starts looking for a GPS signal to work out your current location. The tiny compass at the top left of your Hudl's screen shows that GPS is active. Google Maps zooms in and pinpoints your current location with scary accuracy.

Next, type the address you want to go to. Unless the destination is somewhere very near your current location, Maps usually shows you the distance and travelling time by car (see Figure 11-10). If there's likely to be much variation in how

long a journey takes, Maps usually labels the journey as 'in
light traffic'. Sometimes, you see a warning about congestion,
which appears on the map as a warning triangle.

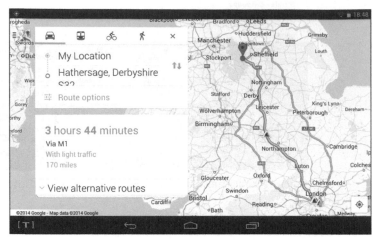

Figure 11-10: Google Maps shows you the fastest route to your destination
by car, train, bus or bike or on foot.

If you don't like the route that Maps suggests or want to try
to avoid possible congestion, tap Route Options. You can also
specify Avoid Tolls and/or Avoid Motorways to see alternative
roads to use.

If you want to travel by public transport or bike or on foot
instead, tap the pertinent icon at the top left of the map to have
Maps recalculate the route and journey times. If you tap the train
icon, you get information covering all forms of public transport.
If you tap Depart at [time], you can specify arrival time, check
the last train home or get information for another day. Tapping
Options takes you to the settings, where you can specify or
exclude particular modes of transport.

To see the Google Street View of somewhere, type the address or place name; then tap the red marker to zoom in and see a navigation photo map of the place. If you tap the arrows, you'll even be able to travel along the street (see Figure 11-11).

Figure 11-11: Google Street View provides photos of where you're going.

# 12

# Shopping on Your Hudl

. . . . . . . . . . . . . . . . . . . . . . . . . . . . . . . . . . . . . . . . . . . .

### In This Chapter

▷ Shopping online securely

▷ Buying groceries and other goods online

▷ Comparison-shopping on your Hudl

. . . . . . . . . . . . . . . . . . . . . . . . . . . . . . . . . . . . . . . . . . . .

*T*he Internet could have been invented for shopping. It's an always-open shop front with an endless array of tempting goodies. No wonder online stores make it so easy to order with just one click. Shopping online is particularly convenient if you live a long way from the places you want to buy from.

Also, web purchases are better protected than high-street ones. If you shop online, you've an unassailable right to return your unused goods, whereas items bought in-store can't be returned just because you changed your mind about them. Of course, it's important to check you're buying from a legitimate business before you give your card details at an online shop. I explain how to make these checks in this chapter.

## Making Secure Online Payments

Because you're typing your payment details into an online form and transmitting them over the Internet, it's natural to worry about who can see your bank information and who's receiving it at the other end. Whenever you shop online or give out your address and bank information, it's vital that you check that the site you're visiting is secure. You can be fairly confident that the big-name companies you're likely to buy from have websites that use a secure server to shield your personal information from prying eyes. On these sites, transactions are encrypted so that they can't be intercepted and your bank details can't be used for other purchases.

In most cases, you can tell that a website is secure because the web address begins with https:// (the *s* stands for *secure*) rather than simply http://. On some sites, you may find a sign somewhere on the home page stating that the site is secure, along with an indication of which company manages its security. Thawte, eSecure and Verisign are the most common logos you'll find on secure websites.

# Keeping Your Bank-Account Info Secure

Because it's so convenient to browse online stores on your Hudl, it can be tempting to check your bank balance to make sure that your account is healthy enough to withstand a shopping spree. This isn't a big issue if you're at home or in the comfort of your hotel room when you decide to log on to your online bank account, but I strongly advise against doing so at an Internet café or somewhere you've gone to make use of the free Wi-Fi.

Wi-Fi hotspots aren't always secure, so anything you send over email or to a website could potentially be intercepted. The risk is small but not worth taking. Public Wi-Fi locations and places that offer customers free Wi-Fi access also attract people who snoop over other people's shoulders and note their passwords and other details. As you can imagine, typing the complex password for your bank account in public is a very bad idea.

# Using Alternative Payment Options

You don't always need to get out your bank card and type your card details into a website. Using a payment service instead can be safer, as you aren't directly giving out your bank account information.

✔ **PayPal:** It's useful to check whether a site accepts PayPal, which is a service set up especially for making secure online payments. You set up an account at www. paypal.com and add funds to it when required. Then, when you want to buy something online, you can do so using your PayPal account number. The advantage is that if someone finds out your PayPal account information and uses it, he or she won't also be able to access your main bank account.

If you prefer, you can simply use PayPal as an alternative payment method. In this case, you link your PayPal account with your bank or credit card account and use PayPal to make the payment, so that you don't end up giving out your bank card details. You can download a PayPal app from the Google Play Store. The PayPal app shows you which local businesses accept payments (see Figure 12-1).

✔ **Dedicated credit card:** Some people prefer to use a separate credit card account with a low spending threshold for online purchases. Doing this has the added benefit of preventing you from overspending.

Using a credit card for purchases over £100 means that the purchase is automatically secured, so if the goods don't arrive or you have trouble obtaining a refund, you'll be reimbursed by the credit card company. Comparable debit card protection is soon to be introduced in the UK but isn't available yet.

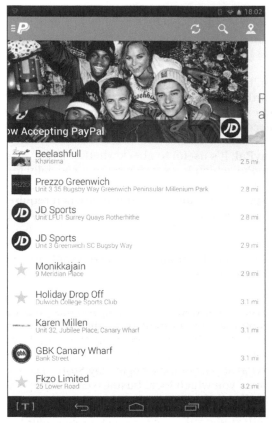

Figure 12-1: You can use PayPal to shop at many online stores.

# Ordering Groceries and Other Goods Online

Now that you know the precautions you need to take when shopping online, it's time to shop!

## Doing your weekly grocery shop

A link in the bottom-left corner of the Hudl's screen takes you to any of the Tesco services and shops you want to use, including the Tesco Direct catalogue and F&F clothing store.

You might want to start by ordering some groceries. Tap the [T] icon and swipe through the screens that appear until you see the Tesco Groceries link. If you're looking for food inspiration, there's a link to a page of recipes that you can browse here. This option also appears while you're shopping at the online Tesco Groceries store, so just tap Shop to go to the online supermarket.

You need an account to shop from home. Log in with your Tesco Groceries account information if you've shopped online with Tesco before; if you're a first-time shopper, tap Register and then complete the onscreen instructions.

When you're logged in, you can start your grocery shop, check what you chose in your previous orders and book a home delivery slot or set up a click and collect slot.

## Browsing items

To start shopping, just browse the neatly categorised list of items in stock. To add an item to your basket, tap it; to add more of the same, tap the plus button (+).

If you change your mind about an item, just tap the item again and then tap the minus button (−) to remove it from your shopping basket. You see a running total of Clubcard points earned and the cost of your order on the left (see Figure 12-2).

Figure 12-2: Clubcard points are shown alongside the cost of your Tesco Groceries order.

Items you have purchased before are listed in the Favourites section, so it's worth checking there for basics you may need. There's also a search field at the top of the screen. Also, the Tesco Groceries site indicates any multi-buy deals and particularly good savings.

 If it's easier, you can tell your Hudl what to look for by tapping the microphone that appears when you tap the magnifying glass. Tap the microphone again, and speak your request.

## *Arranging for delivery or collection*

Next, you need to choose whether to have your groceries delivered to your home or to a local Tesco store for collection. You pay a small delivery charge for either option. Delivery costs the same regardless of the size of your order. If you prefer to collect your grocery order at a local store, tap Click & Collect, and the Hudl will find the nearest Tesco stores where you can pick up your order.

If you opt for home delivery, tap to choose your delivery slot (see Figure 12-3) and then confirm your order and payment details. Afternoon and late-evening slots are usually cheaper than morning and weekend ones.

| DELIVER TO | What time would you like your delivery?<br>Please select a delivery slot from the calendar | | | | | | |
|---|---|---|---|---|---|---|---|
| | | | | Jan 7 - 13 | | | Jan 14 - 20 |
| **Home** | TUE 7 | WED 8 | THU 9 | FRI 10 | SAT 11 | SUN 12 | MON 13 |
| We can reserve your chosen delivery slot for 2 hours. | 7-8AM | £4 0 | £4 5 | £5 5 | £6 0 | £6 0 | £4 5 |
| Please note: when booking your | 8-9AM | £4 0 £4 0 | £4 5 | £5 5 | £6 0 | £6 0 | £4 5 |
| delivery slot, someone over the | 9-10AM | £4 0 £4 0 | £4 5 | £5 5 | £6 0 | £6 0 | £4 5 |
| age of 18 must be available at the delivery address for | 10-11AM | £4 0 £4 0 | £4 5 | £5 5 | £6 0 | £6 0 | £4 5 |

Figure 12-3: You can choose a delivery slot that you find convenient for your groceries.

## Shopping at other Tesco stores

If you tap the [T] icon at the bottom left of the screen again, the Tesco World app will launch, showing you more Tesco stores and a whole host of Tesco services you might be interested in. Tesco Direct is the online catalogue where you'll find lots of useful items for your home. Next to the Tesco Direct link is a link to the page on the Tesco Direct site where you can buy accessories for your Hudl, such as volume-limiting headphones that are safe for children to use.

You'll find a more extensive list of electrical items at Tesco Direct. Tap the Shop by Department bar at the top left to browse by category. When you've logged in to your Tesco account on your Hudl, you can check the balance by tapping Launch on the Tesco Clubcard screen of the Tesco widget.

The Tesco link on your Hudl also takes you to the F&F fashion store, Tesco Bank and the Tesco Phone Shop. There's also a useful Store Locator link.

## Shopping at other websites

You can use the browser to visit and shop at other online stores on your Hudl. To do so, tap the browser icon on the Favourites bar and then type the web address of the online shop you want to visit.

It can be a lot more convenient to use an app created for the shop in question, if one is available (see 'Using shopping apps' later in this chapter). Many online stores have free apps that you can download from the Google Play Store, so try searching for your favourite stores there.

## Bookmarking items to buy later

To save a web page you want to return to later, tap the star at the end of the web address to open the Add Bookmark box. If you want to, you can overwrite the web address and change it to something more memorable, such as 'cool red shoes' (see Figure 12-4). Then tap Save to create the bookmark.

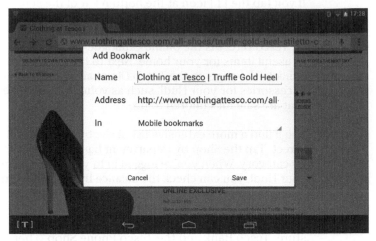

Figure 12-4: Impulse purchases can be a bad idea, but you can bookmark product pages to come back to later.

To see your bookmarked pages, tap the top right corner of the browser bar to open the menu and then tap Bookmarks.

# Getting the Best Online Deals

The web is a great place to find bargains. You don't always need to visit website after website to find the best deals either.

Your Hudl supports *tabbed browsing,* which allows you to have more than one web page open at a time. Tabbed browsing makes it easier to flick between online stores and compare prices and delivery costs for similar items.

To open a new web page, just tap the + button next to the address bar in Chrome. When you leave one page and tap another site's tab, the original web page remains open, so you can go back and forth between the two pages.

# Searching for deals with Google

Another way to check for good deals online is to get Google to tell you where to look. Just follow these steps:

1. **Type a product name in the Search field in the Google app.**

   The search result lists related product prices and websites (see Figure 12-5).

2. **Tap Shopping at the bottom of the page.**

3. **Use the Sort menu at the top right to sort the search results by price, such as low to high.**

You don't always have to go looking for good deals, however. You can get regular alerts about discounts on sites such as Groupon (www.groupon.com) and LivingSocial (www.livingsocial.com), or you can flick through the latest deals by using these sites' apps.

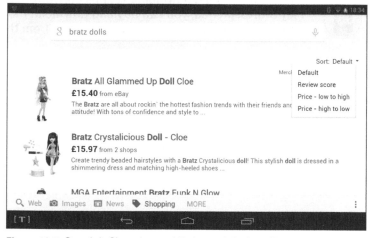

**Figure 12-5:** Google's Shopping tool finds good deals online.

## Using shopping apps

Shopping apps can be faster to use than the website for the same store because the pages load faster. You can find shopping apps easily by typing 'shopping' into the search field in the Google Play Store.

Most goods are competitively priced online, but you should use only those shopping apps you know are secure. Some websites that also offer apps for Android undercut the price of seemingly equivalent apps that you need to pay for through the Play Store. Unfortu-nately, these alternative app sites aren't always secure, so you could be giving your card details to people who will then take more money from your account.

The other danger is that the app you want can be installed only if you enable *rooting* on your tablet — a process that allows apps to install themselves within the Android software and then take over your Hudl.

I advise buying and downloading apps only through the Google Play Store. After all, you can buy and download thousands of apps and millions of books, songs and films from the store.

# Ten Troubleshooting Tips

*L*ike anything else you come to depend on, the Hudl may not always behave quite as you expect it to, or you may be flummoxed by how to do something on it.

In this chapter, I address some of the issues you might encounter and how to fix them.

You can get lots of useful information about using your Hudl at the Tesco website. Just go to www.tesco.com/hudl, and tap the Hudl Help button.

## Keeping Your Hudl Powered Up

Your Hudl should have plenty of power to last for the best part of a day if you use it for a combination of surfing the web, sending and receiving email, using apps and playing music and videos. Even if you watch three blinkbox films on the trot, you shouldn't run out of power before the final credits roll.

Even so, if you're planning a duvet day with your Hudl for company, it's best to make sure you start off with a full battery. You can check how much power you have by dragging down the Quick Settings menu at the top right. The percentage of charge left is listed below the battery icon.

Here are a few ways to keep your Hudl's battery running
for longer:

✔ **Turn off unused connections.** Your Hudl will run longer
on battery power if you remember to turn off the Wi-Fi
and Bluetooth connections when you don't need to use
them. Tap Battery in the Quick Settings menu, and you'll
see a breakdown of what's using the battery the most
(see Figure 13-1).

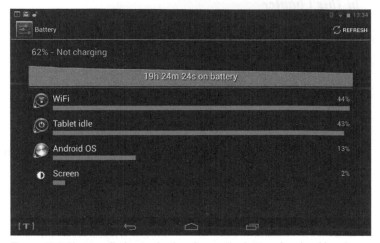

Figure 13-1: You can find out what's using up the battery by checking the
Battery menu.

✔ **Shut down idle apps.** It's also worth keeping an eye
on how many apps you've got running and how much
battery power they're using. You can see what's running
by tapping the Recent Apps button at the bottom of the
Hudl's screen. To switch off apps that aren't needed, tap
Settings⇨Apps⇨Running, and tap End for any apps you
no longer want to run, or swipe the app up to remove it
from the Recent Apps screen.

✔ **Charge only when necessary.** If your Hudl begins to
run low on power, it displays a message saying 'Please
Connect Your Charger'. You shouldn't keep your Hudl
constantly on charge, though, because the process of
running down the battery and then recharging it keeps
it conditioned. Over time, a constantly charged battery
runs down faster than one that's charged only when
necessary.

✔ **Keep it comfy.** Extremes of temperature aren't good for your Hudl (or any other gadgets you own). Don't store the device next to a radiator that's always on or leave it lying in full sunlight for hours.

# Switching On a Stubborn Hudl

Press and hold the power button until the Hudl star appears. This may take a few seconds. If nothing happens and you've charged the Hudl recently, try plugging it into a different socket; sometimes the power source is at fault.

If the Hudl still won't switch on, you may need to reset it. You can do this by inserting the end of a paper clip into the reset button on the top left side of the Hudl's rear (see Figure 13-2). After about 15 seconds, the Hudl should come back to life and restart itself. You won't lose anything you've saved on your Hudl or any of your apps as a result of resetting it.

Reset button

Figure 13-2: You can reset your Hudl by inserting a paperclip into the recess on the rear.

# Staying Up to Date

Updating your Hudl can help clear problems. Your Hudl checks for updates periodically and when an update is available a star will appear in the Notification tray. Tap this star to start the upgrade.

You must have at least a 30 percent charge remaining on your Hudl to upgrade. It's best to plug your Hudl into the mains before starting an update, and also make sure you have a stable Wi-Fi connection so the new software can download.

If there is no star in the Notification tray there still may be an update available as it may have been added since your Hudl last checked. To check manually, swipe down from the top right and tap Settings. Scroll down to About Tablet and tap Hudl Updates. Tap Check Now to see if any updates are offered, and you will be able to download any that are available.

# Backing Up Absolutely Everything

It's wise to back up your Hudl by copying the photos and videos you've taken on it to a computer (if you have one) or by saving them to Google Drive. (See Chapter 11 for details on how useful Google Drive can be.)

If you lose your apps and anything you've downloaded through them, you can download them again for free, if needs be.

# Unsticking a Frozen Screen

If your Hudl screen becomes unresponsive, you can often make it start working again by pressing the power button to put the screen in standby mode, pressing the button again to wake it up and then typing in your PIN or password or swiping the screen to unlock it.

If this trick doesn't help, it's likely that an app has made your Hudl crash. In this case, switch off your Hudl, wait a minute or so and then turn it on again. If your Hudl was working properly until you started using a new app, that app probably caused the crash. Either the app is badly written or it doesn't have enough RAM (operating memory) to run. You can do either of two things:

- ✔ **Adjust the Hudl's available RAM.** You can check how much available memory your Hudl is using by tapping Settings⇨Apps⇨Running. The blue bar at the bottom of the Running screen indicates how much RAM is being used by apps that are running. Android usually stops services that aren't actively being used so that the ones you are using keep running smoothly. If you prefer to, you can close apps you aren't using by tapping each one in turn and then tapping Stop.

- ✔ **Uninstall the app.** If you prefer, you can go to the app's page in the Google Play Store and uninstall it. Whenever you go to the Play Store and search for an app you've installed, you get the choice to Open or Uninstall that app. You can always reinstall any apps you uninstall later, as it's still associated with your account.

 The problem may not always be an app: Screen protectors can interfere with the Hudl's ability to recognise your input. If you're using a screen protector, try peeling it back and checking whether the touchscreen becomes responsive.

# Tracking Down Missing Apps

With the Hudl's multiple Home screens and a wealth of apps and books to explore, keeping tabs on everything that's installed on your Hudl can be tricky. You can usually find something you've misplaced by using the Google Search tool at the top left of the screen, as long as you have Tablet Search enabled (see Figure 13-3). To check, tap the menu at the bottom of the search page; then tap Settings and check that Tablet Search is ticked.

If a Google search doesn't yield results, search the Google Play Store instead. The missing app should be the first result. When you tap it, you'll see an option to open it.

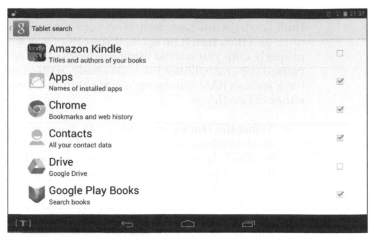

Figure 13-3: You can often find missing apps on your Hudl by using Google.

# Stopping Apps from Sharing Your Information

Whenever you install a new app on your Hudl, you see a message listing everything that the app wants permission to access. You can limit app permissions by installing only apps that don't ask to post messages or share information about you. Here's how:

1. **Go to the Google Play Store's Apps page.**

2. **Tap Settings⇨Content Filtering.**

3. **On the Content Filtering screen, tick Medium Maturity.**

   As well as blocking over-18 content, this option blocks apps that make excessive access demands.

4. **Type** security **in the Apps search box, and choose a free security app from the search results.**

   Kaspersky, Norton, F-Secure and Symantec are all good choices. These apps alert you whenever you try to install an app that wants to access and share your details.

Most security apps also allow you to run a scan to audit the permissions you've already given away to installed apps. You may want to uninstall apps that you find intrusive.

# Securing What's On Your Hudl

It can be very worrying if your tablet is lost or stolen. As well as the financial loss, you may lose everything stored on it, and other people may gain access to sensitive information. Here are a few tips that can help protect the information on your Hudl:

- ✔ **Set a device password or PIN.** It's harder for a thief to access data on a Hudl that requires a password or PIN, so make sure that you add one before you go any further (see Chapter 2).

- ✔ **Change your app passwords.** If your Hudl is stolen, you should change your email password immediately. Anyone who tries to open your email will be prompted to type the new password.

Change your Google password, too (assuming that it's different from your email password), so that associated services can no longer be used on your Hudl.

- ✔ **Recover data from Google Drive.** If you set up Google Drive, as I suggest in Chapter 11, you'll be able to sync your photos and videos to a computer and recover them from there if you need to.

- ✔ **Revoke offline access.** If you set up offline access on your Hudl (see Chapter 11), you can revoke it on your computer so that anything that you shared with your Hudl is no longer available on it. Items that you down-loaded to the Hudl will still be accessible on it, however.

- ✔ **Wipe your Hudl.** You can put your mind at rest by wiping the contents of your Hudl remotely if you've downloaded the paid version of Lookout (https://www.lookout.com) from the Google Play Store. You can view your Hudl's last known location on a map or make it 'scream' its presence (see Figure 13-4). You can also set up a remote wipe. Log in to your Lookout account, select your Hudl and then type your password to confirm that you want to wipe the device's contents.

Figure 13-4: You can trigger an alarm remotely if your Hudl goes missing.

# Keeping Your Hudl Connected

You need a good Wi-Fi signal if you're to be able to get online and to stream music and video to your Hudl. If you've lost the connection, try these quick fixes:

✓ **Reset the connection.** You can lose a Wi-Fi signal if your Hudl has been in standby or idle for a while. In this case, you may just need to remind the Hudl to look for a Wi-Fi connection. Pull down the Quick Settings menu and tap Wi-Fi; then tap the network you've been using. The Hudl should reconnect automatically.

✔ **Plug in.** If your Hudl's battery is very low, any active Wi-Fi connection eventually switches off to preserve power. If you can, connect the Hudl to a power source and then try reconnecting.

✔ **Get closer.** Sometimes it helps to move the Hudl closer to the Wi-Fi router and then try reconnecting. Thereafter, your Hudl should stay connected unless you move out of range.

✔ **Toggle Wi-Fi on the Hudl.** If there's no blue in the Wi-Fi fan, no Wi-Fi signal is available (or Wi-Fi is switched off on your Hudl). Try toggling Wi-Fi off and on again in the Wi-Fi Settings menu. This trick should force your Hudl to reconnect. If it doesn't, you probably have no available Wi-Fi to connect to.

✔ **Try tethering.** In a pinch, you may be able to use Wi-Fi Direct or Bluetooth to get your Hudl online via a laptop or smartphone that's already connected. You need to ask the other person's permission to connect (if it's not your device), and you may not be able to stream music or download large files, but you will be able to check your email and browse the web. For details on how to get connected this way, see Chapter 4.

# Documenting Problems

If you encounter a problem on your Hudl and the cause isn't immediately obvious, it's a good idea to take a screen shot of any error message that appears. Then you can show this screen shot to anyone who tries to help you fix the problem.

To take a screen shot, press the power and volume down buttons at the same time. After about a second, you hear a click, the screen flashes momentarily and you see a preview of the screen shot that has just been saved.

It can be tricky to get the screen-shot feature to work first time. Your Hudl saves each shot, so don't worry too much if getting things right takes a few goes.

# 14

# Ten Ways to Customise Your Hudl

*O*ne of the compelling things about the Hudl is how flexible and open to customisation it is. You can change the appearance of everything on your Hudl so that it looks like a different device. In fact, if you share your Hudl, it makes sense to distinguish between accounts by giving each person's Hudl account a distinctive look. The chances of a 7-year-old and a 15-year-old having the same aesthetic taste are slim, after all.

In this Part of Tens chapter, I show you ten ways to make your Hudl look and behave just how you want it to.

## Adding Accessories

The easiest and most obvious way to make your Hudl look distinctively yours is to add accessories, such as these.

> ✔ **Case:** If you've got a Hudl with a black exterior and want something jazzier, you can. (There's a very good practical reason for getting a case, too; it protects your Hudl if you slip it into your bag and take it out and about with you.)

Choose from a simple case to change the Hudl's overall appearance or get a folio case that flaps over like the cover of a book and also protects the screen. You may want to get a bumper case such as the one shown in Figure 14-1 so you don't have any qualms about handing over your Hudl for your child to use.

To see the range of cases for the Hudl, including ones that double as stands, tap the Tesco Direct widget on the Hudl's Home screen.

Figure 14-1: Protect your Hudl from bumps by putting it in a bumper case.

- ✐ **Earphones:** Listening to music and audiobooks and watching blinkbox movies is a much more immersive experience if you're wearing headphones. If you want your child to listen to storybooks on the Hudl, I recommend using child-friendly headphones which have a built-in volume limiter.

- ✐ **HDMI connector:** Add a micro-HDMI cable to your Hudl and the whole family will be able to watch blinkbox movies and Clubcard TV programmes on your HDTV.

# Changing the Wallpaper on Your Hudl

If you've had a look at Chapter 6, which is all about photos, you know that you can use any photo stored on your Hudl as the background image, or *wallpaper*.

Here's a quick way to change your wallpaper:

1. **Tap and hold an area of the screen that has no apps on it.**

   The Choose Wallpaper From menu appears.

2. **Tap the option you prefer.**

   If you choose Wallpaper, you see the wallpaper options that the Hudl came with. If you choose Gallery or Photo, you get to flick through your own photos.

3. **Tap the wallpaper or photo you want to use.**

   The Hudl displays it full-screen.

4. **Tap the item again, tap the vertical menu bar at the top right and tap Set Picture As (see Figure 14-2).**

   You'll see crop marks around the photo. Slide your finger across the image to adjust which parts are cropped out and then tap Save.

Figure 14-2: Add your own photo as the background wallpaper to your Hudl to instantly distinguish between user accounts.

You can also choose 'live' wallpaper, which has a constantly changing background. To install a live wallpaper you can use the method I described above to select items already on your Hudl; tap Live Wallpaper to see the selection. You can also search for 'live wallpaper' in the Google Play Store. Add a topic such as 'sea' or 'space' to narrow down the search results, if you want. When you see a wallpaper you like, tap to select and install it, and then tap Open to launch it. Use the wallpaper Settings option to specify how often the image changes.

 Some wallpapers contain annoying adverts for other apps, some of which may not be suitable for children. If you're downloading a live wallpaper to use on your child's Hudl account, make sure you look thoroughly at any extras it tries to draw your attention to. If you aren't happy, close the app, go back to its page in the Google Play Store and tap Uninstall to delete it.

# Using Widgets to Customise Your Screens

Your Hudl has lots of fun widgets that you just need to drag onto an available screen to use. You can add a mini gallery to your Hudl screen, for example, by using the Photo Gallery widget. To do this, tap All Apps in the Favourites bar, tap the Widgets tab and swipe through the widgets until you spot the Photo Gallery. Tap and hold this widget, and it appears on one of the Hudl's screens. When you're asked to choose a photo source, select an album, individual photo or Shuffle All. Now you can flick through your photos without having to open the Gallery to see them.

Scan through the Widgets tab to find more useful and popular widgets, such as the digital and analogue clocks, which place large clock faces on the Hudl's screen, making it much easier to check the time. There are also widgets for Google Calendar, Email, Directions, Google Drive and more.

# Organising Apps and Widgets

In Chapter 3, I introduce apps and widgets, and show you how to move them between screens. It's a good idea to keep apps and widgets of a particular type, such as communication or music, on the same screen.

You can also store related apps together within a folder to make them easier to find. To group your apps, drag them to the same screen and place them near one another; then drag one of the app icons to another app icon of the same type. A blue glow appears around both icons. When you take your finger off the screen, the two icons appear in a folder labeled 'unnamed'. Tap this word, and when the keyboard appears, type a label. Figure 14-3 shows a folder I created for music apps. To add more apps to the folder, drag their icons over to it.

Figure 14-3: Place apps of a similar type in folders to make them easier to find.

# Using Widgets as Shortcuts

When you install some apps, you also get a widget that you can use to quickly change how the app behaves or to access its tools without having to tap around within the app. If you

install an app such as Spotify (www.spotify.com) or BBC
iPlayer (www.bbc.co.uk/iplayer), it's worth checking your
Widgets screen (tap All Apps⇨Widgets) to see whether you've
got a widget for that app. If you have, drag it to one of the
Hudl's Home screens to access its extra controls.

# Changing Your Hudl's Launcher

You can make everything on the Hudl's screen look com-
pletely different by using another launcher. The *launcher*
dictates how the buttons and menus look and how they're
arranged (see Figure 14-4).

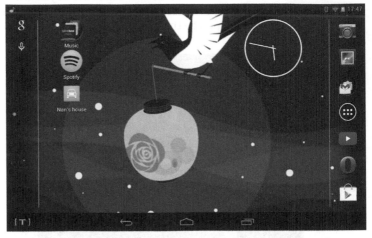

Figure 14-4: You can change the look of your Hudl by installing a different
launcher and lock screen.

Some fun launchers, such as GO Launcher EX, are available
in the Google Play Store, so browse through them and try out
any you want to.

When you install a new launcher, your screen-lock settings are
deleted, so you need to set up a new screen-lock password
(see Chapter 3). GO Launcher prompts you to install its GO
Locker screen lock app, but other launchers don't warn you
that you need to add a new password lock.

# Replacing Your Browser

Although Google's Android software runs your Hudl, you don't need to use Google's services for everything. If you'd prefer to use a different search tool or a different web browser, you can. The Opera Mini web browser, for example, is a good alternative to Google's Chrome browser.

You can download Opera for free from the Google Play Store. As the installation completes, Opera will load a screen of 'favourite' websites including BBC News, Google Search, Wikipedia and Opera's Sports news site. You can change any of these entries by tapping on them and typing in the web address of site you want to use instead. There are also two blank slots so you can add more sites to the 'speed dial' page of websites you can visit with a single tap from Opera's start page.

Once you've got Opera (or your browser of choice) set up as you want it, you can choose to make it your default browser — this means it will be the browser that launches every time you go online. The easiest way to do this is to remove the Chrome browser from the Favourites bar and replace it with Opera.

1. **Hold your finger on the Chrome icon and drag it to the top right of the screen.**

   An X will appear. Now lift your finger off the screen. Chrome will be deleted. You'll still be able to use it as it's still installed — just tap All Apps and you'll see it in your Apps menu.

2. **Now find the Opera icon. Hold your finger on it and drag it into the space on the Favourites bar that Chrome has left empty.**

   Now when you want to surf the web you just tap in the same place as before.

If you decide you preferred Chrome after all, you can easily reinstate it by dragging Chrome out of the All Apps menu and back into the Favourites bar. If you want to, you can keep both browses in the Favourites bar. Just drop Chrome onto the Opera icon to create a folder containing both items (as I describe in 'Organising Apps and Widgets' earlier in this chapter) and name the folder 'browser'.

# Making Multiple Search Engines Available

The Google Search tool is a fixture at the top left of the Hudl's screen, but that doesn't mean you can't use a different search tool — or several. You could use Microsoft's Bing (www.bing. com) when you're searching for images, for example, as Bing specialises in image searches.

You can keep your search options open by installing the Search Engines app from the Play Store, which provides links to all the most popular search engines (see Figure 14-5). Tap the one you want to use for the search you're about to start.

Figure 14-5: Google doesn't have all the answers. Sometimes you'll get better results if you use a different search engine.

# Changing Your Input Options

Although the touchscreen keyboard generally is easy to use, there may be times when you find it easier and faster to use a real keyboard instead. Fortunately, you don't have to look hard to find a keyboard you can use with your Hudl; all the main electronics shops sell Bluetooth keyboards. For details on pairing a device with your Hudl via Bluetooth, see Chapter 4.

You can also use a digital pen or stylus to write on your Hudl's screen. These items cost only a few pounds and are intentionally simple to use, which makes it much easier for you or your child to use the Hudl as a drawing pad (see Figure 14-6).

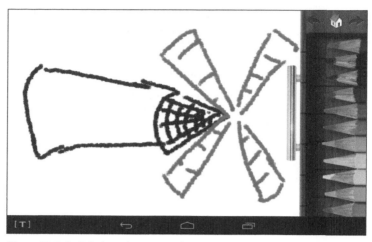

Figure 14-6: A digital pen lets you write on your screen rather than having to constantly tap items.

# Making Your Hudl's Screen Easier to Read

As well as decluttering your screen by organising your apps and widgets into folders, you might appreciate larger text to make books and emails easier to read.

- ✔ **Larger text in ebooks and magazines:** If you use your Hudl for reading, you can find options to increase the text size and reflow the page layout (see Chapter 9).

- ✔ **Larger text in emails:** You can also increase the text size of emails you receive. To do this, tap Email⊅General⊅ Message Text Size, select a larger text size and tap the screen again to dismiss the options. When you go back to your email inbox and tap any message, you'll see that the text is larger.

- ✔ **Larger menu and app labels:** You can increase the text size of all the menus and app labels on your Hudl. To do this, drag down the Quick Settings menu at the top right, tap Settings⊅Display⊅Font Size and then tap either Large or Huge.

✔ **Larger keyboard keys:** You may find it helpful to install a keyboard with larger keys. Big Buttons (available from the Google Play Store) is a good choice, because it shows you a magnified view of each button as you tap it so you can be sure you've tapped the right item.

✔ **Brighter screen:** You can adjust the screen brightness by choosing Brightness from the Quick Settings menu and then choosing a new brightness setting.

# Index

### • F •

### • G •

# About the Author

**Rosemary Hattersley** is a technology and small business journalist who has been writing about tablets and smartphones for the past decade. For many years, Rosemary was a stalwart of *PC Advisor*, writing and commissioning features, reviews and how-to guides on most sorts of consumer technology. She has also worked for *Computeractive* and has been a regular contributor to *Macworld* as well as a number of consumer technology websites.

She co-authored the third edition of Wiley's *iPad For the Older and Wiser* and has edited and co-authored several *Complete Guides* for IDG covering Android, iPad, iPhone and Windows. As well as an impressive collection of smartphones and tablets, Rosemary hoards digital radios and cameras — in other words, she's a classic gadget girl.

Follow Rosemary at www.twitter.com/rosiehattersley.

# Dedication

For Lou, my partner in gadget appreciation. xx

# Author's Acknowledgments

It's been fantastic to be able to work on *Hudl For Dummies*. Thanks to Craig Smith and Ellie Scott at Wiley for commissioning me to write it, and to the Hudl and blinkbox teams at Tesco for creating a hugely successful and robust Android tablet with bells on. Particular thanks are due to Sara Shlaer and Kathy Simpson for their editing, patience and invaluable guidance. Thanks too to James Peacock, for his painstaking technical editing work, and to Tim Warren and Garry Blackman for their insight into the Hudl's unique apps.

# Publisher's Acknowledgments

**Executive Commissioning Editor:**
Craig Smith

**Senior Project Editor:** Sara Shlaer

**Development and Copy Editor:**
Kathy Simpson

**Technical Editor:** James Peacock

**Editorial Assistant:** Anne Sullivan

**Project Coordinator:** Melissa Cossell

**Cover Photo:** Tesco Stores Ltd

Lightning Source UK Ltd.
Milton Keynes UK
UKOW07f1511020115

243841UK00001B/1/P